IMAGES OF WALES

PONTYPRIDD
A MARKET TOWN

Market Street, September 1972. There has been a market in Pontypridd since 1805, mainly for country folk to sell and barter their wares. In 1860, a new market – at first in its own hall but soon spilling out into the streets – began attracting shoppers from far and wide and Pontypridd, then known as Newbridge, became known as 'the Petticoat Lane of the Valleys'.

IMAGES OF WALES

PONTYPRIDD
A MARKET TOWN

DEAN POWELL

The History Press

First published 2005
Reprinted 2014

The History Press
The Mill, Brimscombe Port,
Stroud, Gloucestershire, GL5 2QG
www.thehistorypress.co.uk

British Library Cataloguing in Publication Data.
A catalogue record for this book is available from the British Library.

ISBN 978 0 7524 3578 7

Printed in Great Britain.

Contents

	Introduction	7
one	A Frontier Town	9
two	A Heartland of Industry	59
three	A Cultural Capital	91

This book is dedicated in loving memory to the author's grandparents, Tom (1909-1973) and May (1903-1997) Powell of Oakland Crescent, Cilfynydd. Also to their three sons who have gone before us: Don (1928-2001), Billy (1931-1939) and Alan (1936-2004) who loved this town.

Don, Billy and Alan Powell outside their home in Oakland Crescent, Cilfynydd, 1939. Their nephew, author Dean Powell, was born in Llantrisant and is both a Freeman and Trustee of the town. He graduated from the University of Wales College of Swansea with a Bachelor of Arts degree in English and Welsh and is now Editor of the *Pontypridd & Llantrisant Observer* and Literary Editor of the *Western Mail*. He makes frequent appearances on TV and radio as a guest speaker. A member of Treorchy Male Choir for seventeen years, he is their regular compère and tenor soloist and has undertaken a series of successful tours to Canada, America and Australia, where he performed in venues throughout Perth, Brisbane, Melbourne and at the Sydney Opera House. Dean is also their Publicity Officer and Honorary Archivist. This is his fifth book for Tempus.

Introduction

Pontypridd was a remarkable frontier town, born out of the industrialisation of its surrounding valleys and transformed from a sleepy agricultural region into one of the most populated in Wales. Undoubtedly, its incredible growth was due to two hugely important factors: firstly its proximity to the Glamorganshire Canal, allowing an easy route between industrial Merthyr and Cardiff, and secondly the coming of the Taff Vale Railway, this time linking the docklands to the rapidly expanding Welsh coalfield in the Rhondda. Together they gave Pontypridd the foundations to develop into a major market town which blossomed at the very heart of industrial South Wales.

The first major development to take place in the vicinity was the building of a magnificent bridge in 1756 by local stonemason William Edwards. On his third attempt he succeeded in his aim to allow farmers easy access over the Taff by creating an architectural splendour, portrayed by a variety of artists who flocked there to gaze on his splendid achievement, nothing less than the longest single-arch bridge in the world. Although it did little to change the rural character of the district, the bridge led to the growth of a small cluster of houses on either side of the Taff and the area was named Newbridge. It was another century before the town was renamed Pontypridd. The original was probably Pont-y-ty-pridd (bridge of the earthen house), which is thought to refer to a small hut which may have stood near the eastern bank of the river.

By the end of the eighteenth century, the first phase of industrialisation in Newbridge was under way. The most significant event was the opening of the Glamorganshire Canal in 1794. Before then, coal had to be carried from Merthyr to Cardiff in wagons over rough tracks. In the next three and a half years, workmen sliced through a 25-mile channel and the canal became a vital component that turned Newbridge into a major municipal centre. By 1818 Ynysangharad Works, a chainworks, was opened, marking the first major industry to come to the area due to the canal.

The next phase of industrialisation began in 1840 with the Taff Vale Railway which, like the canal, ran from Merthyr to Cardiff. No one had anticipated the enormous growth of the Rhondda coal industry which followed the opening of a level at Gyfeillion, a mile from Newbridge, by Dr Richard Griffiths in 1790 and another by Walter Coffin at Dinas in 1807. Turning the lush green Rhondda into something of a vast black Klondike, those early mining pioneers penetrated indiscriminately into the valley floor for their precious black gold. It was an event which had a tremendous effect on Newbridge, as the town found that it was ideally placed for transporting coal to the docks. As the region produced most of the coal and iron on which the economy of the British Empire depended, the peak of production in 1913 saw 57 million tons of steam coal pass through the town to Barry and Cardiff. Pontypridd had the longest railway platform in Britain in an effort to cope with its 500 trains and 11,000 passengers per day. Newbridge became famed for its open-air market and gradually its commercial prosperity made it the shopping centre for the valley communities.

The pace and extent of the growth of the town in late Victorian and early Edwardian times was breathtaking. By 1839, Newbridge had acquired a police force and in 1850 it had lighting in the main streets. A County Court met in 1851 and the town had 1,000 homes and 33 public houses. In 1856, the first post office opened and the town changed its name to Pontypridd, largely due to a decision by the local postmaster. During the same year, a father and son who worked at a local woollen factory had a profound effect on the musical history of Wales. Evan James and his son James penned a haunting Welsh hymn which was eventually named 'Hen Wlad Fy Nhadau' and became the national anthem of their homeland.

During the twilight years of Victoria's reign, Pontypridd's status as a major market town and urban area was strengthened. Following the widespread growth of Nonconformism and the building of many chapels, St Catherine's church was built in 1869, complete with its domineering spire overlooking the bustling town. The first newspaper was established in 1873 and by 1885 there was a horse-drawn tram service, closely followed by the electric tram and trolleybus. A new Town Hall was built in 1890 and a public library opened its doors. In 1905, the Municipal Building was opened for Pontypridd Urban District Council (PUDC) and in the middle of the town a charming fountain was erected. The town played host to the National Eisteddfod of 1893 and established its own County School in 1896. The town's population had grown from 2,200 in 1847 to a staggering 38,000 in 1899.

With the passing of the First World War, Pontypridd folk dug deep in an effort to pay their respects to those who had given the ultimate sacrifice for freedom. No better monument could have been erected in their honour than the opening of Ynysangharad War Memorial Park in 1923, the jewel in Pontypridd's crown. Culturally, the town continued to blossom, particularly in the fields of choral singing and opera. World-famous Sir Geraint Evans and Stuart Burrows were born in the same street in neighbouring Cilfynydd and the town's choirs achieved worldwide fame. In contrast, Pontypridd's best-known musical artist in recent years, Tom Jones, has continued to spread the good name of his home town. In the sporting world, Pontypridd produced world-famous boxers, cricketers, swimmers and of course its incredibly popular rugby team, which was formed way back in the late 1870s.

Sadly, today Pontypridd bares the scars of deterioration, visible neglect and an irresponsible series of planning errors, leaving this proud market town a different Pontypridd from its heyday in the Victorian era. Yet despite the many changes, seen all the more clearly when examining many of the photographs in this collection, our beloved 'Ponty' remains a unique town and one we hold so very dear to our hearts. Long may this continue.

Dean Powell
March 2005

The author would like to thank Hywel Matthews of Pontypridd Library, Brian Davies of Pontypridd Museum and the work of the late Don Powell for help in compiling this book.

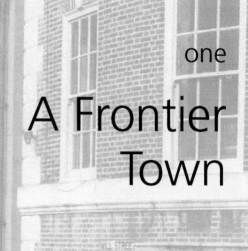

Engraving of Newbridge, *c*. 1830. Playwright and poet Gwyn Thomas described Pontypridd as 'the hub of sophistication, a town poised genially in an intermediate state of grace'. He was referring to the town's location in a broad bowl between Llanwynno and Llanfabon, the two mountains and parishes on either side of the Taff Valley, and to its position halfway between the old coal and iron townships of Rhondda, Cynon and Merthyr and the city of Cardiff.

Craig yr Hesg and the River Taff with Trallwn to the right. The pace and extent of the growth of Pontypridd in late Victorian and early Edwardian times was breathtaking. The population grew from 2,200 in 1847 to 15,000 in 1861, 20,000 in 1891 and some 38,000 in 1899.

Pontypridd viewed from the Common. In its first industrial phase during the last years of the eighteenth century, Pontypridd had many of the hallmarks of a frontier town, growing from a sleepy hamlet into one of the biggest towns in Wales. In 1913, at the peak of production, 57 million tons of steam coal passed through Pontypridd on its way to the docks in Barry and Cardiff, by then the biggest coal-exporting port in the world.

A view of Pontypridd, 1930. By 1839, the town of Newbridge, a lawless and disease-ridden place, had its own police force, consisting of a sergeant and six constables. In 1850 it had a Gaslight and Coke Company, which was responsible for lighting the main streets. A County Court met at the White Hart Hotel in 1851 and by 1852 the town had 1,000 houses and 33 pubs.

Pontypridd from Common.

The River Taff from the Old Bridge, with Berw Road on the left and Zion Street on the right and the Welsh Congregational Chapel, built in 1870. In 1856 the first post office opened and in the same year the town changed its name from Newbridge to Pontypridd, largely because the postmaster, Charles Bassett, had grown tired of having to deal with mail intended for the many other Newbridges in Britain and Ireland.

Opposite above: Pontypridd from the Common, showing the Glamorganshire Canal and Brown Lenox chainworks. In 1901, Pontypridd had three woollen factories and mills taking water from the Taff and Rhondda, several breweries, a chemical works, a vinegar works, brickworks and flour mills, as well as shops and offices galore in its busy main thoroughfare, Taff Street.

Opposite below: Pontypridd, clearly showing the Tumble and the Sardis Chapel in the centre. Boasting a popular open-air market, Pontypridd also benefited from its canal linking it to Merthyr and Cardiff, its railway line, bustling streets and a municipal life of its own. Ponty, as it became affectionately known, was indeed becoming a major town in the South Wales valleys during the second half of the nineteenth century.

Next page: Pontypridd, *c.* 1970.

The junction of Berw Road, Bridge Street and Taff Street, 1964. Further along Berw Road, which eventually leads to Glyncoch and Ynysybwl, was the Ruperra pub. Directly opposite the Bridge Inn can be seen the corner of Tabernacl Chapel.

Taff Street towards Bridge Street, with the Palladium cinema on the left, c. 1910. The crowds hustle and bustle across the tramlined street as they visit an array of busy shops on Taff Street.

Left: Old Toll House, Taff Street, 1963. Once a toll-house leading to the cattle market, Robert Smyth opened a 'chemist, wines and spirits' there in April 1889. The tower was built on the corner of Turnpike Lane (also known as River Street and Ford Street), which led to the former cattle market. It later became Crosswell's wine shop and off-licence. The building was demolished when the Taff Vale shopping centre was opened in the mid-1960s.

Below: Taff Street. The YMCA and Palladium cinema were on the left. In late Victorian days, shoppers threaded their way through crowds swarming in and out of the shops. Also, they walked among the horse-drawn wagonettes or brakes arriving at the market from Cilfynydd and Ynysybwl and the hansom cabs darting to and from all parts of the district, with laden tricycles and bicycles and whistling errand boys hurrying here and there with their delivery baskets.

Garfield's sports store, Taff Street, December 1963. This was one of several properties on Taff Street that were demolished to make way for the new Taff Vale shopping precinct. Notice the fashionable wrought-iron balcony above the shopfront, which ran the length of this part of the street.

Peglers', Taff Street, December 1963. The shop and its adjoining properties were demolished shortly afterwards and another unique building in Pontypridd was lost forever.

Tredegar Arms, Taff Street, December 1963. This picture was taken a matter of months before the demolition crew flattened this section of Taff Street. In 1850 the pub was kept by Thomas Williams, later to be succeeded in the 1860s by Thomas Evans.

The demolition of properties at the north end of Taff Street, 1964. The concrete monstrosity of the Taff Vale shopping precinct opened in the late 1960s but within just twenty years had become a run-down eyesore in the town.

Taff Street, 1964. The properties along the north end of Taff Street have been completely demolished to make way for the new Taff Vale shopping precinct.

Taff Street following the demolition, 1964. On the opposite side of the road was the Fine Fare supermarket, once the Palladium cinema, and the YMCA next to it, where Pontypridd Athletic Club regularly trained.

Taff Street, facing south towards the Fountain. Notice the pawnbroker's sign (three balls) on the right at No. 34 Taff Street; a sign for the shop owned by Arthur Faller. Shoppers would dodge the butcher's carts speeding along High Street and Taff Street. They met the street-hawkers, the bell-ringing muffin man on the corner of the New Inn, the Shoni-onion man with his beret and his bike, and Tom Marshman's (Old Tom Cockles') cart.

Taff Street. In spite of the savage economic decline experienced by Pontypridd in the 1920s and '30s, the market has survived in very much its original format. The Market Company has resisted the temptation for wholesale development, opting instead for gradual refurbishment of the original buildings, retaining both indoor and outdoor markets in their traditional style. Since 1985, it has undergone considerable change. The Lesser Town Hall was refurbished and opened as a market hall in 1988, and the outdoor market was extended in 1988 onto a site adjoining Church Street and St Catherine's Street.

Penuel Square, with Penuel Calvinistic Methodist Chapel in the centre and the Town Hall set back on the right, 1899. This was a familiar area for temperance speakers to address the crowds over the years. Cambrian Lane, a market entrance roadway running beside Penuel Chapel, was known as Occupation Road. It was an appropriate name, as many craftsmen worked there from the 1840s in the little cottages and workshops and in the bordering area where the New Town Hall was later built.

Penuel Square facing north, showing such well-known stores as Rubens and Halewoods. On the right-hand side, at No. 56 Taff Street, the Pontypridd Urban District Council opened its first offices in 1895.

Left: The Fountain, 1895. Canopied with Celtic interlace and inscriptions, the four drinking bowls were designed by C.B. Fowler. The stone drinking fountain was unveiled in 1895 by its donor, Sir Alfred Thomas, MP for East Glamorgan (later Lord Pontypridd). It was designed to provide fresh drinking water to passers-by and animals. The relief inscriptions on the undersides of the projecting bowls read: 'Duw a Digon / Heb Dduw Heb Ddim' (God is Everything / Without God Without Anything).

Below: Penuel Square and the Fountain, *c.* 1910. Horse and carts and trams were the main forms of transport through the busy market town when this photograph was taken towards the end of the Edwardian era.

Taff Street and the rear of Penuel Chapel, *c.* 1890. The Hopkin Morgans shop, now the Princes café, is on the right, with C.G. Roberts' Ironmongers on the corner and the Tea Exchange further along.

Taff Street and Penuel Square, 1927. The Thomas & Evans store is on the left, alongside W.R. Noyes the fruiterer, and chemist T. Ernest Jones.

Taff Street, 1967. By the time this picture was taken, Penuel Chapel had been demolished, making way for the Fraternal Parade shops. Other shops in the immediate vicinity include Oliver's, Millets, Haines and Roath Furnitures on the left, with their favourite slogan: 'A Square Deal All Round'.

Taff Street, branching into Market Street to the right. The Pontypridd Markets, Fairs and Town Hall Co. was incorporated by an Act of Parliament in 1877. Lands of the old marketplace and buildings such as the corn market, china warehouse, shops, workshops and offices were purchased from Clara Thomas and George William Griffiths Thomas by local businessmen who became directors of the new company.

Left: The entrance to Market Street from Taff Street, 1963. It is widely believed that a phantom known as the Ghost of Market Square lived in a house in Tyfica Road for some years of his Victorian lifetime. His apparition was first encountered one night in Market Square in 1902. Late one night, the ghost was glimpsed leaving the rear of the New Inn Hotel by the Arcade entrance. A watcher at one of the high windows looking out over the rear courtyard stables of solicitor neighbours Morgan, Bruce and Nicholas saw the ghost looking up at the building for several minutes, before it moved towards the hotel and simply faded away.

Below: Taff Street and Market Street, *c.* 1950. Edgar Fennell was the longest established fishmonger in Pontypridd and kept breakfast tables served with kippers at a penny a pair and supplied rabbits for a shilling – although he faced great competition from local poachers who stalked the woodlands and hillsides of the district with snares and guns.

Market Street, with Penuel Chapel graveyard on the right. A market has been held on the same site since 1805. The present market was built following the incorporation of the Pontypridd Markets Company.

Market Street, 1904. The indoor market sold mainly agricultural produce from 1805 and during the same year the corn market moved to the corner of Church Street from Llantrisant. One of the stalls in 1882 was run by Gwendoline and Benjamin Gibbon from Ystradowen, who sold butter, bacon, eggs and meat from their farm. The famous Arcade, which linked Market Street with the lower end of Gelliwastad Road, was built in 1886.

Easter Market, Market Street, 17 April 1935. Opposite is the Cambrian Studio, run by Thomas Forrest, a photographer in Pontypridd for nearly forty years. He took an interest in the newly developing art while he was employed at the Brown Lenox chainworks at Ynysangharad. Also on the street was F. Day, leather and grindery merchants, Stead & Simpson and the New Inn at the farthest end.

Market Square, c. 1920. The Victorian architecture of Market Street and Church Street is seen in the high buildings of yellow brickwork decorated with red-brick patterns. The Co-operative Movement was attracted to the area in 1898 and the Co-op came to Market Square, eventually taking over the whole of the Arcade until 1984, when it was demolished.

Market Street, c. 1950. The large building halfway up on the left is Market Chambers, with the Scudamore butcher's shop on the corner of Church Street. The next large building along was known as the Silver Teapot building and now houses the Market Tavern.

Market Street, and Church Street to the right, c. 1910. Pontypridd's most famous pub, the stylish New Inn Hotel, can be seen in the background. To the right was the Arcade.

Cowboy Starr selling handbags at three for half a crown in Pontypridd market, December 1949. Probably the most familiar of the market salesmen in Pontypridd was cockle-seller Tom Marshman. Known affectionately as Old Tom Cockles, he began selling cockles in the district when he was just fourteen, obtaining his supplies from relatives in Kidwelly. His horse and cart and cries of 'Cockles Kidwelly, good for the belly' were part and parcel of the culture of the Graig, where he lived for most of his life. Tom had a wooden leg and the tale goes that if he rode with his leg inside the cart it was going to rain. However, if it hung outside the cart as he travelled along it was a sure sign of fine weather to come!

Taff Street, c. 1910. Pictured during a quiet shopping day in the main thoroughfare that runs through the town, running parallel to the River Taff on the right.

Taff Street, *c.* 1880. This picture wonderfully grasps the air of Victorian confidence in Pontypridd, which had grown from a relatively unknown agricultural area into a thriving market town.

Taff Street, *c.* 1910. To the left is the New Inn Hotel and opposite is the Park Hotel, now the site of the Woolworths store. Also on the right was the Butchers Arms Hotel, which became part of the Park Hotel.

Building Messrs Thompson and Shackell's New Music Salon, 1890. In 1900, at Barry Road, a nineteen-year-old woman was murdered by her Jamaican husband, William Lacey, and he became the first black man to be hanged in twentieth-century Britain. The couple married on Easter Tuesday 1900 and moved to Pontypridd. The relationship between them was a stormy one, not helped by Lacey's jealousy. On Friday 6 July 1900, a ferocious argument took place at their home. Finally, a scream was heard and when the landlady checked on the couple, she found Pauline lying dead. A bloodstained razor was close to the body. Lacey walked to the police station and confessed to the killing. Lacey was executed, aged twenty-nine, on Tuesday 21 August 1900 at Cardiff.

The Butchers Arms Hotel, later occupied by the Midland Bank, *c.* 1970. Originally called the Masons Arms, probably from when it was one of the small cottages that sold ale, it was rebuilt several times to a bigger size. The words 'Butchers Arms Hotel' can still be seen set in stone lettering just below the gable roof of the bank. When exactly the Masons became the Butchers is unknown, but already there was a small market taking place behind it which rivalled the small cattle and corn market that was running alongside the New Inn on the opposite side of the road. In later years it became part of the Park Hotel, by which time billiard tables made their first appearance in the town, and the Welsh Professional Billiards championship was held there in 1914. The Butchers Arms was the venue for the inaugural meeting of Pontypridd RFC.

Mill Street, with the National Provincial Bank Ltd on the right, *c.* 1963. Mill Street bustled with craftsmen from the early Victorian era. In medieval times it was a rough track to Llanwonno, passing Gelly Fynaches Farm and the convent above Graigwen. With the coming of the railways in 1840, the Taff Vale Railway bridged the River Rhondda upstream and an arch on the bank near the Welsh Harp spanned the road, overlooking a watermill in the field below.

Mill Street, c.1960. The street derived its name from various mills in the vicinity, such as the Rhondda Flour Mill. This was the main road to the Rhondda before major changes took place to the traffic system in Pontypridd in 1967.

Mill Street, c. 1960. A busy little street branching off from Taff Street, this is also the home of the Celtic Club, a well-known drinking establishment in the town – but for men only!

The New Inn, *c.* 1900. Originally a farmhouse dating from the 1730s, with a thatched roof, it later became the premier hotel in the town, boasting a magnificent staircase by 1922, built for £750 with a view of the grand stained-glass window beyond. In May 1857, the New Inn was taken over by John George Cousins and, under his tenancy, the pub's Long Room, later called the Assembly Room, was where petty sessions of Llanwonno and Ystradyfodwg were held. The building was extended in 1893 but sadly demolished in 1981 to make way for a series of shops.

The Park cinema during severe flooding of the River Taff, *c.* 1955. The Park was one of a whole host of cinemas in the town, including the Palladium, the Town Hall, the County and the White Palace, all with two shows a night changed twice weekly. Originally an open space behind the Park Hotel (or Butchers Arms), it was used by showman Jacob Studt for his Easter Fair, which included the biograph (the earliest form of cinema) accommodated in a tent. The Park cinema finally closed its doors on 14 December 1957.

Building the bridge between Ynysangharad War Memorial Park and Taff Street, 1923. The original footbridge was built in the summer of 1897 and it was proposed to build it opposite the Arcade from Market Square but instead the lane next to the Butchers Arms Hotel was chosen. In 1923 a concrete bridge was built, only to be severely damaged by flooding and rebuilt in October 1991.

High Street, looking towards Taff Street and the corner of Mill Street, 1890. This picture clearly shows the iron parapet of the bridge over the River Rhondda. The building protruding onto the pavement to the right was the Temple of Fashion. On the corner of Mill Street is one of John Crockett's shops.

Taff Street, c. 1965. By the time this photograph was taken, Marks & Spencer had opened their new store on the right-hand side. It was built over the River Rhondda, as were other shops which later appeared on the left.

High Street, showing the Half Moon Hotel in the centre, the Empire Musical Hall entrance on the left and the Royal Clarence Theatre on the right. The Clarence Theatre was built in the 1890s and became the first permanent theatre, in the South Wales coalfield, with the ability to seat an audience of 1,000. Built by John Trenchard and later run by Byron Charles, it was fitted with gas lighting, therefore ensuring a total ban on smoking inside. It was renamed the New Theatre and extended in 1901. Further extensions took place in 1938 when it became the County cinema.

Next page: An aerial photograph of the south end of Taff Street, c. 1960. This marvellous view of the street was taken from a rooftop on High Street. It shows the bridge over the River Rhondda in the foreground and the curve of Taff Street towards the Gwilym Evans store. Also notice the large gasometer on Gas Lane in the background, which was demolished in the 1980s.

The Tumble, or Station Square, showing the original Clarence Hotel and the well-known Two-Foot-Nine on the right, *c.* 1900. The tram road was built by coal pioneer Walter Coffin in 1810 from his collieries at Dinas. They linked with Dr Richard Griffiths' tramroad from Gyfeillion Colliery near Hopkinstown to a private canal at Treforest and the Glamorganshire Canal at Dynea, allowing the coal to be transported to Cardiff.

The Tumble, with the White Hart pub on the right. Public houses have played a major role in the history of the town and there's always been a huge variety to choose from. Some of the familiar inns included the Volunteers, Bluebell, Half Moon, White Hart, Cross Keys, Clarence, Greyhound, Criterion, Bunch of Grapes, Victoria, Castle, Taff Vale, Horse and Groom, Wheatsheaf, Prince of Wales, New Inn, Butchers Arms, Maltsters, Ivy Bush, Bridge Inn, Tredegar Arms and Somerset.

The Tumble, showing the new Clarence Hotel, built in 1912. This view shows Taff Street on the right and Sardis Road bus terminus to the left. William Morris of the Welsh Harp once rented the Clarence Hotel and, to encourage custom, established a collection of monkeys in the bar.

The Tumble, c. 1940. The White Hart is on the left, followed by the Greyhound, a well-known haunt for local boxers. Also pictured is the old post office with the Half Moon pub and Amelia's on the right.

The Tumble was once the busiest coal-dram centre in the country. Horse-drawn drams travelling from the collieries at Penrhiw, Gyfeillion, Gelliwion and Dinas 'tumbled' coal into the larger drams headed for the Doctor's Canal at Treforest. Throughout the nineteenth century, the Tumble was the heart of the town, becoming a centre for its most popular inns.

Tumble and Sardis Road. Tailor Syd Hoffman's shop was on the left, followed by the White Palace cinema. The greater majority of this street was demolished in 1991 in an effort to create an inner relief road which aimed to free Pontypridd from further traffic congestion. It failed.

Sardis Road towards the Tumble, c. 1967. At the time, Sardis Road was closed at one end, allowing buses to turn and park at the terminus alongside the County cinema to the left.

The Welsh Harp on Rhondda Road, September 1907. It was once the home of the *Pontypridd Observer* newspaper. The first newspaper, the *Pontypridd District Herald*, was established in 1873, followed by the *Pontypridd Chronicle* and, in 1897, the *Pontypridd Observer*, which is still essential reading for the people of the town and district.

Staff of the *Pontypridd Observer, c.* 1954. During the 1870s, Archibald Allan McLucas established the *Herald*, which was printed in Mill Street. Benjamin Davies bought it out to create the *Chronicle*, which in turn was purchased by the Glamorgan Free Press. The first issue of the *Observer* was printed on 20 March 1897 and cost a halfpenny. It later had an office and printing works at No. 77 Taff Street and was edited by Percy Phillips up until the Second World War, when he was killed in a road accident.

Mill Street sports ground, with Carmel Chapel to the left of centre. The majority of this area has been completely transformed with a series of new roads in an effort to rectify the traffic problems associated with Pontypridd.

The Colliers Arms Hotel and Caddy electrical shop in Mill Street being demolished as part of the redevelopment of the town in 1967.

A view of St Catherine's church and the rear of Mill Street from Sardis Road, *c.* 1967. The run-down buildings give an almost Dickensian feel to the town.

The redevelopment of Pontypridd, 1967. Substantial alterations were made to this area of Pontypridd in an effort to loosen the bottleneck which had developed when Mill Street was the sole gateway to the Rhondda.

The redevelopment of Pontypridd, 1967. Sardis Road was opened for traffic following these major changes to the road system, which led to the demolition of a number of buildings along Sardis Road junction and Mill Street.

The start of Gelliwastad Road, showing the police station on the right and the Co-operative Arcade to the left, *c.* 1965. The police station was built on the corner of St Catherine Street in 1868. Commanded by Supt Jabez Matthews of Berw Road, by 1884 the force consisted of eight officers. The police force expanded to meet the needs of the population and by 1895 there were seventeen officers. A new police station was opened on the junction of Berw Road in 1984 and the old station was eventually demolished in 1990.

Pontypridd Library and the road leading to Graigwen. The first library in Pontypridd was built in 1890, costing £2,400, of which £900 was raised through public subscription.

Gelliwastad Road, facing St Catherine's church. One of the most prominent offices was that of Spickett's solicitors, originally based in Courthouse Street. James Edward Spickett was born in Pontypridd in 1859 and his father was the first registrar of Pontypridd. In 1899 James took over the role for a further forty-two years and, with the help of his chief clerk, Walter Morgan, he recruited youngsters from the town to launch a local rugby team. In 1878 they held a meeting at the Butchers Arms Hotel and at the age of seventeen James became the first captain of Pontypridd RFC.

Gelliwastad Road, facing the Municipal Buildings. On the left is the current Gelliwastad Institute. Originally, the Gelliwastad farmhouse was part of the Thomas estate. It was presented to the town by Miss Clara Thomas and opened by her in 1899 as the Institute.

Gelliwastad Road, c. 1920. The imposing late-Victorian development of Gelliwastad Road and Gelliwastad Grove, centring around St Catherine's church, was designed to house the professional and business people of Pontypridd. Today it remains the hub of local solicitors and accountants.

The Municipal Buildings, Gelliwastad Road. The district council offices were built in 1903, costing £23,000 and designed by Henry T. Hare of London, who entered a competition. The distinguished building displayed an air of Edwardian self-confidence with its triple-arched entrance. It was the new home of the Pontypridd Urban District Council, formed in Taff Street in 1895.

Pontypridd fire brigade, formed in 1890. Originally, the brigade operated from a shed in Penuel Lane and its equipment consisted of a hosereel, six 50ft lengths of leather hose, a horse-drawn engine with manually operated piston pipes and a ladder. By 1894, an electrical communication device from the police station was installed and sent warnings to the firemen's houses. In 1897 there were nine of them, commanded by Capt. Arthur Owen Evans of Berw Road, and two years later they moved to a new headquarters in Gas Lane.

Morgan Street, now the site of Pontypridd bus station, pictured in March 1967. This is another area of Pontypridd long since forgotten and demolished under the banner of 'progress'.

Matthews Court, with Morgan Street in the background, pictured on washing day in the 1920s. The houses were demolished in the 1960s and the present-day Pontypridd bus station occupies much of this site.

Chapel Street with the Taff Vale shopping precinct tower in the background, 1967. Notice the children walking home from Lanwood Schools – this was a well-known shortcut into town.

A view towards the Berw Road junction across the old bridge from the Maltsters, 1939. The Bridge Street shops are on the left-hand side, with an advert for the White Palace cinema on the side of Marenghi's café.

Berw Road, *c.* 1910. This picturesque postcard shows Craig yr Hesg mountain in the background and a pretty tree-lined street overlooking the River Taff.

Craig yr Hesg and Berw Road. Many of the old buildings in Pontypridd are decorated with fine stonework and constructed mainly from locally quarried stone. Craig Yr Hesg quarry is still producing the distinctive blue pennant stone, which, with its granite-like hardness, ensures that a large amount of the best buildings will survive for many years to come.

Marenghi's and the Old Bridge Café on Bridge Street, December 1963. They were torn down to make way for the Taff Vale shopping precinct. Fortunately, a photographer had the foresight to picture many of the buildings in Pontypridd before they were lost forever.

The Old Bridge Pharmacy on the corner of Bridge Street and Taff Street, December 1963. The building was later demolished.

The Ivor Arms Hotel, Bridge Street, which was renovated in 1907. An alleyway by the pub led to Ivor Court, adjacent to Llewellyn Court which was a group of houses on land that is now part of the miniature golf course in Ynysangharad Park. The buildings were demolished in 1936.

Trallwn Bridge to Pontypridd viewed from the Corn Stores, 1902. Between the bridge and the lock-keeper's house on the left was Canal Place. This was the canal gateway to Pontypridd and within the vicinity were three inns: the Queens Hotel, the Crown Hotel and, hidden by the lock-keeper's house, the Llanover Arms.

Trallwn Bridge, at the foot of Corn Stores Hill which connected the centre of Ponty with the old Cardiff Road through Coedpenmaen. The road ran adjacent to the canal at this point, behind William Lewis's corn stores, built in 1850 and seen here beyond the lock.

Opposite below: Dr William Price (1800-1893). Chartist, surgeon, heretic, archdruid and pioneer in the legalisation of cremation in the British Isles, Dr William Price was undoubtedly one of the most flamboyant, romantic and eccentric characters in Welsh history. Born in Rudry in 1800, he became a rather brilliant scholar, studying at The London Hospital and becoming a surgeon by the age of just twenty-one. In 1827 he became the surgeon of the Brown Lenox chainworks. Claiming to be the Archdruid of Wales, he was often seen carrying out ancient Druidic rights on the Rocking Stone (Y Maen Chwyf). A leader of the failed Chartist Rising of 1839, he fled to France disguised as a woman. In 1860 he built the Round Houses at Glyntaff as the entrance to his new home and museum to Druidism, but the venture failed. Known for his flamboyant headdress and costume, he opened one of the first co-operative societies in the town and was also responsible for an embryonic national health service for the workers. In 1871 he moved to Llantrisant with his housekeeper, who was sixty years his junior, and the couple had three children. The first, named Iesu Grist (Jesus Christ) died after five months and Price attempted to cremate the corpse, causing mayhem in the town. In March 1884 he conducted his own defence at the Cardiff Crown Court trial over the cremation, claiming it was not right to allow a carcass to rot in the ground and pollute the earth. He was acquitted by Justice Stephens, making way for the passing of the Cremation Act of 1902. After sipping a glass of champagne, Price died at the age of ninety-three and was cremated in Llantrisant. A crowd of 20,000 turned out for the event and a carnival atmosphere prevailed throughout the town.

Above: Common Road, leading to the site where Pontypridd Golf Club was opened in 1905. The Common was a well-known meeting place for large crowds, who often came to listen to political or religious speeches. When, in 1857, coalowners reduced wages by 15 per cent, several thousand miners in Pontypridd and the Rhondda called a strike and met here to listen to the strike leaders unveil their plans. Hordes of blacklegs stormed into Pontypridd by train and descended on local collieries to work the pits and troops were called in to maintain order. The strike was quickly broken and hungry miners were forced to accept the coalowners' terms.

Myfyr Morgannwg (Evan Davies). Born in January 1801 near Pencoed, he received no formal education and devoted himself to the mastery of the Welsh bardic rules and the study of mathematics. At first he called himself Ieuan Myfyr and began to preach in Congregational Chapels near his home. A clockmaker by trade, he settled in Mill Street, Pontypridd in 1844 and came deeply under the influence of the Druidic fever sweeping the town. Myfyr won the chair at the Pontypridd Eisteddfod in 1854 for the Welsh ode 'The Sacred Circles of the Bards' and held Druidic ceremonies at the Rocking Stone until 1878. He published several books dealing with Druidism and was appointed to adjudicate essays in the Llangollen Eisteddfod of 1858. He died in Pontypridd on 23 February 1888 and was buried with copies of his publications placed under his head. His grave, also occupied by his wife Sarah, was a few yards from the entrance in Glyntaff churchyard, on the right-hand side.

Y Maen Chwyf (the Rocking Stone) on the Common. The Rocking Stone is a large boulder left precariously perched by a retreating glacier. It became the centre of a romantic nineteenth-century resurrection of Druidism. In 1850, Myfyr Morgannwg built a serpent of standing stones around it. It is made up of two concentric circles joined to a winding avenue of stones, ending in a small circle that has the two eyes of a serpent.

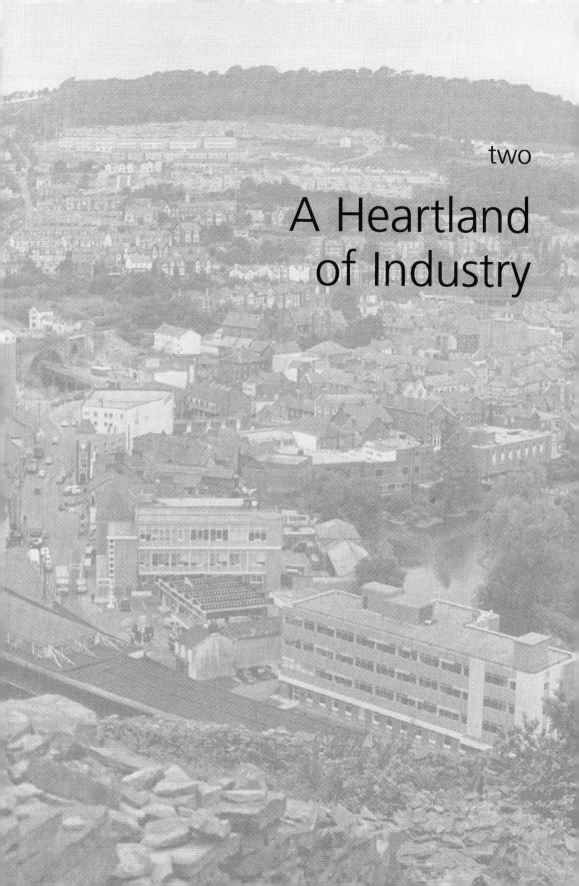

two

A Heartland
of Industry

William Edwards. Born on 8 February 1719, the youngest son of a farmer at Ty Canol Farm on Eglwysilan, William became an expert at repairing and building walls for neighbouring farmers and learned his craft by building several houses, forges and mills in the parish. He apparently took much interest in the great walls of nearby Caerphilly Castle. His greatest legacy was the creation of the famous bridge at Pontypridd. In later years he also built bridges at Aberavon, Llandovery, Morriston, Usk and Glastonbury. His son David built Newport Bridge and others at Bedwas and Llandeilo. William lived for many years at Bryn Trail Farm, high above Glyntaff. After being converted by the famous revivalist Howell Harries in 1739, he became a lay preacher. While building the bridge at Morriston, he also built a chapel there and presented it to the congregation. He was ordained as a Welsh Independent Minister at Groeswen Congregational Chapel and gave his salary to the poor. He held the post until his death on 7 August 1789 and was buried just outside the south door of Eglwysilan church.

Opposite above: 'The Bridge of Beauty' by Julius Ibbeston (1759-1817), depicted from the Graig, 1790. When local farmers despaired at being unable to cross the River Taff at Pontypridd, except when the water level was low enough to use a ford, they commissioned William Edwards to build a bridge for £500. His first bridge was a three-arch structure, built in 1746 and sited slightly downstream from the present bridge. After two and a half years, while William watched anxiously, tree trunks and other debris battered the bridge during a severe flood and it collapsed and washed away. He had pledged to maintain the bridge for seven years and had to reconstruct it. He conceived the idea of a one-arch bridge, a perfect segment of a circle, 35ft high with a 140ft chord or span and a diameter of 175ft. Wheelwright Thomas Williams built a substantial centring to support the arch while it was under construction. Stone for the bridge was quarried locally. However, when the bridge was nearing completion in 1751, it collapsed.

Opposite below: The bridge, as depicted by Michael Angelo in 1795. Following his two failed attempts, Edwards was in debt and discouraged but a subscription of £700 promoted by Lord Talbot and Lord Windsor enabled him to finish the bridge. He did not know the laws of equilibrium or balance, and the pressure caused by the 32ft long by 20ft high abutments, or haunches, of the bridge was so great that after several years the crown of the arch was forced upwards and the central section collapsed. Undaunted, he lightened the weight of the haunches by making three cylindrical openings of 3ft, 6ft and 9ft in diameter in each. The danger that the light curve of the bridge would spring upwards again was avoided. The Old Bridge was started in 1755 and completed in 1756 and was for many years one of the longest single-span bridges in the world. It is believed the three attempts at building the bridge gave rise to the phrase 'three times for a Welshman'.

The Victoria Bridge, opened in 1857. A century after William Edward's bridge was built, the need for a second bridge was greater than ever. The original bridge could not cope with streams of carts and carriages that could barely pass each other. Solicitor Edward Colnett Spickett received letters for the new bridge to be built by Glamorgan Quarter Sessions and public subscription was held. Robert Hughes was the architect and the entire project cost £1,575. Stone was quarried from Trallwn and the bridge was built by Thomas Jenkins.

Opposite above: The two bridges seen from Zion Street. The original William Edwards structure was described as 'a rainbow of lightness, width and elevation of the arch, the beau ideal of architectural elegance, rising from the steep bank on one side of a salmon river and resting gracefully on the other side and situated between the beauty of steep, wooded hillsides'.

Opposite below: The River Taff flooded in December 1960. For years, the river was prone to flooding, often affecting the rear of shops on Taff Street and parts of Ynysangharad War Memorial Park.

The two bridges, 1975. The Victoria Bridge was opened in December 1857 with a grand ceremony which included the Pontypridd Drum and Fife Band and Treforest Brass Band marching across it. In fact, the 'new' bridge was a monumental disaster, totally obscuring the view of the original Edwards bridge from the south.

Brunel's skew-arch stone bridge at Mill Street, 1840. When Brunel built the magnificent stone railway viaducts over the River Rhondda in Pontypridd, the stage was set for the penetration northwards by the Taff Vale Railway Company. Originally, the viaduct – which provided a path for the railway to Merthyr and Aberdare and later to Ynysybwl, Llanwonno, Nelson and Llancaiach – was a single-line skew structure. The main span over the River Rhondda had a width of 110ft and may well have attracted scepticism regarding the stability of such a wide span. Critics were proved wrong, for these viaducts have stood the test of time and carried the weight of trains far in excess of that for which they were designed.

The Mill Street viaduct under alteration in 1904. Anthony Hill of Hill's Plymouth ironworks in Merthyr asked Brunel to estimate the cost of a railway from Merthyr to Cardiff, which was eventually put at £190,649 – and probably included the cost of the skew viaduct at Pontypridd. This request was endorsed, although there was obvious opposition from the Glamorganshire Canal Company – the main artery for transportation to Cardiff – but following parliamentary debate it received royal assent on 21 June 1836. Lady Charlotte Guest laid the foundation stone in 1837.

The White Bridge, Berw Road, 1938. In August 1898, Pontypridd Urban District Council approved the order to build the iron road bridge over the Taff at Berw Road to relieve the severe congestion of carts and carriages using the canal bridge by the Queens Hotel on the road to Cilfynydd. Designed by Hennebique, the French inventor of reinforced concrete structures, it was built in 1907 by L.G. Mouchel and Partners and opened on 6 April 1909. The bridge was reinforced in 1938.

The Machine Bridge, Treforest, arguably one of the world's oldest surviving tramroad viaducts. The origin of the bridge dates back to Dr Richard Griffiths, a local GP who invested in the growing coal-mining industry. He became a major shareholder in the Glamorganshire Canal and saw the potential of building a horse-drawn tramroad from the new coal levels in the lower Rhondda Valley to the canal. That is why he commissioned the building of the original Machine Bridge and tramroad in 1809. It crossed the River Taff to a feeder canal at Dynea which led into the Glamorganshire Canal. This was known as the Doctor's Bridge but was later called Machine Bridge because a weighing bridge was constructed on one end to measure the amount of coal which crossed the river. In 1913, a concrete bridge, designed by Hennebique, was added on to the south side,.

The railway viaduct at Berw Road. This structure, built in 1855, carried the Taff Vale Mineral Line to the Albion Colliery in Cilfynydd. It later carried passenger trains between Pontypridd and Nelson.

A watercolour by John Petherick of the Taff Valley to the south from Ynysangharad, 12 July 1854.
By the end of the eighteenth century, the conditions for the preliminary phase of industrialisation in
Newbridge were under way. The first significant event was the opening of the Glamorganshire Canal
from Merthyr to Cardiff in 1794 – before then, coal had to be carried to Cardiff by mule or in wagons
over rough tracks. A barge could carry 24 tons and was worked by a horse, one man and a boy. The
same amount would take twelve wagons, forty-eight horses, twelve men and twelve boys.

Canal locks in Pontypridd, showing Mr Bladen of Llandaff with Joey the horse in 1936. An illiterate army
of muscle men moved into Merthyr Tydfil in 1781 and literally cut their way through the valleys to shape
the future of South Wales during the Industrial Revolution. Over the next three and a half years, the navvies
cut an astonishing 25-mile channel from Merthyr to Cardiff. The Glamorganshire Canal was a vital link
in a chain of events that turned the valleys from rural retreats into major industrial centres. The Merthyr
ironmasters built the canal to take their produce to Cardiff and other entrepreneurs were swift to see the
potential and sunk pits near the canal and linked up with it by horse-drawn trams. Some of the most intense
activity was around Pontypridd and it changed the area into a bustling industrial town.

The Brown Lenox assembly shop, 1965. At its peak during the Second World War, some 300 workers produced anchor chains for the Royal Navy. Sadly, Brown Lenox closed in 2000 after nearly 200 years in production.

Opposite above: The famous Brown Lenox chainworks, known as the Ynysangharad Works, was established by cousins Messrs Samuel Brown and Samuel Lenox in 1818. It was the first major industry to come to Pontypridd due to the canal. The location of the site provided easy access via the Glamorganshire Canal to supplies of iron from Merthyr Tydfil and Hirwaun and was close to abundant coal and water supplies. Initially, the Brown Lenox works concentrated on supplying chains for the shipping industry but they were also to provide chain links for suspension bridges and engines, trams and shackles for the collieries.

Opposite below: The Brown Lenox chainworks first brought the great British engineer, Isambard Kingdom Brunel (1806-59), who designed the Clifton Suspension Bridge and the three largest ships in the world, to Pontypridd. Among its many customers were the Admiralty, the suspension bridge at Hammersmith, the chain pier at Brighton and Thomas Telford's bridge over the Menai Straits. The firm made chains and anchors for many liners, including the *Lusitania*, the *Mauretania*, the *Queen Elizabeth* and the *Queen Mary*, and for the warships *Rodney* and *Nelson*. When German warships were scuttled at Scapa Flow in 1918, they were found to be equipped with chains and anchors made at Brown Lenox.

Maritime Colliery, Pontypridd. The colliery was opened by John Edmunds in 1841, after he sank a shaft 800 yards deep to the north of Gelliwion Colliery (sunk in 1838) and at a depth of 60 yards found and worked No. 3 Rhondda Seam. From 1875 to 1930, it was part of the Great Western Colliery and became known as the Pontypridd Colliery. A new shaft was sunk in 1906 and by 1920 it employed 1,040 men, dwindling to 412 by 1959. It eventually closed in June 1961.

Albion Colliery, Cilfynydd. The sinking of the two shafts began in 1884 but on 24 March 1886, two men were killed when part of the brick lining of one of the shafts collapsed. A few months later, four more were killed in a similar accident. At 3.50 p.m. on Saturday 23 June 1894, a blast ripped through the colliery, claiming 290 lives and leaving 150 widows and 350 fatherless children. It was the most brutal mining disaster in British history before Senghennydd. The colliery was closed in 1966.

Left: Pwllgwaun Colliery. This photograph shows the winding gear of Dan's Muck Hole at Pwllgwaun Colliery. The colliery, named after mountain fighter Dan Thomas, had a shaft a mere 45 yards deep and was also entered by a level beginning near what is now the grandstand of Pontypridd RFC's ground at Sardis Road. The workforce was never very large, with some fifty-two men producing 1,200 tons of coal in 1937. The colliery was worked from 1873 until 1950.

Below: Great Western Colliery, Hopkinstown. The depth of the colliery was 293ft when it was sunk in 1848 by John Culvert. The colliery was sold to the Great Western Colliery in 1866. Three more shafts were sunk in 1872. On 12 August 1892, an explosion killed sixty-three men and boys and a further sixty were killed on 11 April 1893. The colliery closed in 1923.

A view of Pontypridd, showing the Taff Vale Railway line. Pontypridd was the 'gateway to the valleys', according to the rail company slogan. The railway came to the town in 1840 and, like the canal, ran from Merthyr to Cardiff. It served the district and town until 1922, when it was taken over by the Great Western Railway. When Brunel carried out a feasibility study for the proposed railway in 1836, he assumed that its main function would be to carry iron from Merthyr. No one anticipated the rapid growth of the Rhondda coal trade which followed the opening of a level at Gyfeillion, a mile or so up the valley from Newbridge, by Dr Richard Griffiths in 1790 and of another by Walter Coffin (1784–1867) at Dinas in 1807. But, as the extraction of coal got under way in the years following, the town found that it was ideally placed for transporting it down to the coast, especially as the railway-station, unlike the road and canal, was conveniently situated on the Rhondda side of the valley.

A view of Pontypridd, showing the railway line, 1973. Between 1901 and 1912, the station was totally changed, allowing coal trams to pass through it without stopping. The station was visited by 11,000 passengers meeting 500 trains per day. Pontypridd railway station is still the longest train platform in Britain.

In 1872, work was completed on building a track through rocks which passed under Carmel Chapel and connected directly the Merthyr and Rhondda lines without trains having to go into Pontypridd. The two viaducts and the cutting formed a triangle and at each corner of the triangle was a signal box: at the Pontypridd Junction, near the station corner; Pontypridd Northern, on the Merthyr line; and the Rhondda Cutting Box on the Rhondda branch, which also controlled the entrance to the coke ovens marshalling yard at Hopkinstown. The cutting became known as the Rhondda Cutting or the Pontypridd North Curve and made it possible for up trains to turn around by reversing through the cutting and returning down the Rhondda line via the new viaduct.

The railway line, showing the horses that were used to shunt railway carriages on the line, 1891. At the Rhondda Cutting, an accident took place on 19 October 1878. The Cowbridge train reversed into the cutting, came out the other side and went straight into the Rhondda down train. Carriages scraped along the side and three vehicles disintegrated, one mounting the other and then toppling down again with a fearful crash. Scores of passengers, with blood streaming from wounds in their faces and heads, were lying about the smashed carriages or jammed between them. Legs were severed, passengers were dead or dying and, as a Pontypridd newspaper reporter explained: 'The mass of maimed and crippled humanity presented a sight sickening in its very horrible haplessness and its ruthless destructiveness.' Five were killed on the spot and a further eight died afterwards.

Above: Pontypridd railway line. The next disaster in the town took place in the railway station itself, on 13 August 1891. At 2 p.m., a special train had been provided to take a Volunteer Review from Treorchy back to Pontypridd, Mountain Ash, Dowlais and Aberdare detachments. Arriving at the station, the five carriages stood on the down line when, suddenly, the Merthyr to Cardiff train took the curve into the station. The driver did not realise another train was there and smashed into its rear 'like matchwood, scattering the people on the platform in all directions', according to a report. The back carriage, carrying equipment, lifted onto the platform and dragged along it before becoming wedged against pillars supporting the roof. Some passengers were jammed in the third carriage, which was partly smashed, and other carriages were sent hurtling down the line. Fifteen people were injured, with some having limbs amputated, but nobody was killed.

Opposite top: Early in the morning of 23 January 1911, at the height of the miners' strike, news spread of a rail crash at Hopkinstown. Many were dead and dozens were injured. Among the dead were three well-known miners' leaders, including councillors from Ferndale, Pontygwaith and Treherbert, along with a Methodist minister from Caerphilly. A passenger train from the Rhondda was timed to leave the station at 9.40 a.m. for Pontypridd and Cardiff. While travelling at about 30mph towards the coke ovens, it crashed into a fully laden train from the Lewis Merthyr Colliery, which was stationary on the same track. Passengers were trapped, bodies hung through smashed windows and eleven of the dead were laid in the engine shed.

Opposite middle: Celebrations as the first electric tram is used in Pontypridd, 6 March 1905. A trial run was made over the route on 16 February and the tram service started in March. Special tramcars left from the PUDC offices, then near the Fountain, at 11 a.m. The first tram, filled with invited dignitaries smartly dressed in warm overcoats and bowler hats, was driven by Hugh Bramwell, chairman of the PUDC electricity committee. As electric trams started running between Cilfynydd and Treforest, and between Pontypridd and Trehafod, the age of the brakes gradually came to an end. From late Victorian times, Solomon Andrews & Sons had operated a horse-drawn tramcar service between Pontypridd (Welsh Harp) and Porth with six tramcars and twenty-one horses soon working on the route. The tramway was sold to the British Electric Tramway Co. Fierce opposition to 'danger in the streets' from proposed electrification meant that the horse-drawn trams continued running until April 1902, when service was withdrawn.

Opposite bottom: A tram travelling across the Victoria Bridge. The Pontypridd Urban District Council fought for a publicly owned electric tram service and Acts of Parliament of 1901 and 1902 authorised construction of the tramway. The Board of Trade examined the estimated cost of £60,000 to introduce the service and another £50,000 for a generating station to power the service and the new streetlights. In 1903, the PUDC secured the rights to run the service and a generating station was built next to the gasworks in Treforest, just off Cemetery Road. A tram route was planned to run from Treforest, through Pontypridd to Cilfynydd. The firm of Blackwell started laying the tramlines in September 1903.

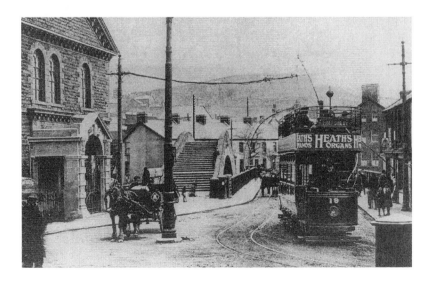

The Tramwaymen Parade, 1912. The Treforest-Cilfynydd tramlines ran from the council depot at Cemetery Road in Glyntaff, down past the Llanbradach Arms to Castle Inn Bridge, over the River Taff and up Forest Road. Single tracks with loop-line passing places ran down Fothergill Street in Treforest and along the Broadway to the Tumble. Broadway, together with Sardis Road, was known as Tramroad. The electric trams continued down High Street past the Clarence Hotel, through the narrowness of Taff Street (with its double tracks), over the Victoria Bridge, up Corn Stores Hill and along Coedpenmaen Road to Pontshonnorton, then to the terminus opposite Albion Colliery.

Brakes travelling through Pontypridd. In 1899, fifty-seven brakes and thirty cabs and brougham carriages were operating in Pontypridd. The hansom cab was a two-wheeled cab for two passengers and many were built at Morgan Street. They had large wheels of some 7½ft in diameter and were drawn by a single horse. The driver sat high up behind the body of the cab and the reins passed over the hooded roof, which had a small trapdoor through which the driver and his passengers could communicate. Entry to the leather interior was through padded knee-doors, or half-doors, at the front. Hansom fares, approved by the PUDC on 22 October 1901, ranged from a shilling to go from the railway station to nearby streets to two shillings or more to go to places further afield. A proposal by the Swansea Motor Omnibus Company in June 1899 to run a Daimler motor car service between Pontypridd and Cilfynydd was rejected and horse-drawn brakes continued on the route.

Transport on Taff Street and Market Street. In December 1923, the PUDC wanted to improve the flow of traffic by having only one tramline in Taff Street instead of two, but two lines in Market Street instead of one – thus making a one-way traffic system through the town. Market Street would be a terminus for the Pontypridd to Cilfynydd section of the tram service. However, the market directors considered that trams rattling through Market Street and Market Square on Wednesdays and Saturdays would be dangerous to all the shoppers and would interfere with the stallholders' rights.

A tramway crash, May 1919. This picture shows a tram from Cilfynydd, which ran out of control down the Corn Stores Hill. It took the bend over the canal bridge by Canal Place and the Queens Hotel, sailed past the Llanover Arms, across the Victoria Bridge and crashed into the William Harris grocery shop on the corner of Taff Street.

Tramway Crash, March 1919. This photograph shows a tram bound for Treforest which toppled as it was leaving Market Square and fell against the corner of the Thompson and Shackell Music Salon (later Gwilym Evans). A tram once left the track and ran into the windows of the Arthur Faller pawnbroker's shop at No. 34 Taff Street.

A Pontypridd bus headed for Cardiff, *c.* 1920. Some petrol-driven buses ran between Cilfynydd and Treforest from Monday 16 June 1930 and seven new trolleybuses arrived in late August. One of the conductors was William Marsh of Treforest, a well-known member of the local fire brigade. If Billy spotted a fire while on duty, he would race off to attend the outbreak and the tram or trolleybus would be stranded until the fire was out or under control.

A tram travelling through Taff Street to Treforest, *c.* 1905. Sunday tram services began on the first Sunday in February 1926 but there was little future in Pontypridd for trams. Having run for twenty-five years, in 1930 they were replaced on the Treforest to Cilfynydd route by trolleybuses. Tramlines were torn up and virtually removed from the whole district by the end of 1933. Operation of tram services from Pontypridd to Trehafod had always been difficult because of frequent road subsidence and flooding on the route beyond Hopkinstown. Petrol-driven buses took over on this route. The tramcars were dismantled and their wooden seats sold at 1s 3d each for use in gardens.

A double-decker bus travelling along Taff Street. The PUDC operated both single- and double-decker trolleybuses and had advantages over the tram in that it was not confined to a track, it loaded and unloaded passengers at the kerbside rather than in the roadway, and was quieter and smoother in operation. Trolleybuses were also cheaper to run than petrol buses and gave off no fumes. The trolleybus could manoeuvre easily and give way to traffic that the tram so often held up in Taff Street.

Two buses travelling in opposite directions on Taff Street. 'With the trolleybus we have got the best of both worlds,' said T.I. Mardy Jones, the local MP, when he inaugurated the Treforest-Cilfynydd service on Thursday 18 September 1930. Hopkin Morgan and Arthur Seaton, both ex-chairmen of the PUDC, assisted him at the ceremony. Initially, the new service could not cope with the demands of the route and for a time some of the trams played nursemaid and ran in conjunction with the trolleybuses. To ensure the prompt departure times of all local single- and double-decker trolleybuses and motor buses, the crews synchronised their watches with the official Transport Department clock, known as the Bundy, set in its green case on a shop wall in the Ynysangharad Park entrance opposite Mill Street.

A double-decker bus outside Burton's, Taff Street. During the war years, bus drivers coped well with the difficulties and hazards of driving in the blackout and keeping to their time schedules. The *Observer* reported that some passengers were taking advantage of the blackout by passing dud coins to the conductor when paying their fares. In 1956, the PUDC decided that the provision of new streetlights and attendant roadworks at Cilfynydd would mean costly alterations to the overhead electricity supply system. The trolleybus service came to a sudden stop on Thursday 31 January 1957.

The cottage hospital on the Common. The hospital was built due to the support of voluntary subscriptions. The site was given by Miss Clara Thomas of Llwynmadoc and the memorial stones were laid by the Viscount Tredegar on 5 May 1910. A carnival was held to celebrate the first hospital in the town, followed by a sports day at Taff Vale Park and a grand firework display. The hospital itself was officially opened by Miss Clara Thomas on 27 February 1911.

St Catherine's church. Work on St Catherine's started in 1866, due largely to the generosity of Miss Clara Thomas, the property and coal-mining heiress, who donated the land and £7,000 towards the construction. It was also helped by a grant from the Church authorities of £175 on condition that everyone in the town was free to worship there. John Norton of London was the architect and William Morgan of Pontypridd the builder. The church was opened in 1868, although the north aisle was added ten years later. The spire of St Catherine's, which rises 162ft above the town and has eight bells, is a distinctive landmark.

Opposite above: Miss Clara Thomas of Llwynmadoc, Breconshire. Miss Thomas was a distinguished and benevolent citizen of Pontypridd and heiress to the Griffiths property and fortune. She was one of the descendants of Thomas Thomas and Jane Griffiths of Llanbradach. Her love of Pontypridd was obvious, as she supported the building of both St Catherine's church and the cottage hospital during her lifetime. Miss Thomas died on 12 June 1914.

Opposite below: Interior of St Catherine's church. St Catherine's was John Norton's immediate successor to Norton church in Neath and equally dominant in the town, with its elegant spire, clock face, lofty nave and lower chancel. The walls were built out of rough Newbridge sandstone with Bath stone dressings. Norton – responsible for Cilfynydd's Pontsionnorton Bridge and many fine buildings in the UK, India and Africa – was chosen for the prestigious project. He is thought to have taken Keble College, Oxford as his inspiration, in collaboration with ironmasters' builder Arthur Seaton.

Penuel Calvinistic Methodist Chapel, opened in 1812. The Town Hall, now covered by a concrete frontage, is on the right in Penuel Lane. It became the entrance to the present-day fruit and vegetable market. The bingo hall, which later opened above it, was closed in 1987.

Rear of Penuel Chapel, 1966. The graveyard and chapel were demolished a year later to make way for the Fraternal Parade shops.

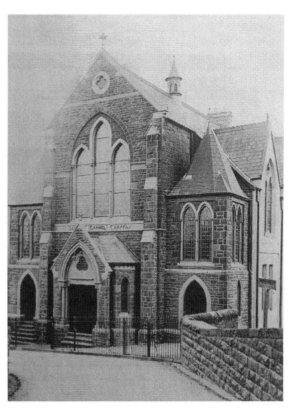

St David's Presybyterian church, Gelliwastad
Road. It was built in 1883 by Henry C. Harris
of Cardiff. In 2002, it joined forces with the
congregation of the United Reformed church.

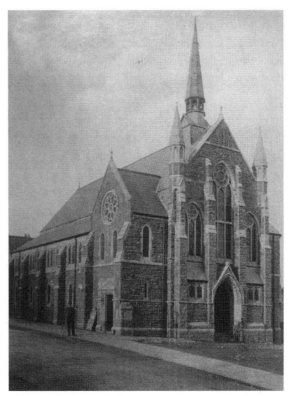

United Reformed church, Gelliwastad Road.
The church dates from 1887 and was built as
an English Congregational church. Part of it is
now used as a shelter for the homeless.

Wesleyan Chapel, Gelliwastad Road. Built in 1848 as a chapel and school and designed by local architect Arthur O. Evans, the site is now home to the Muni Arts Centre, a thriving theatre and cinema.

Capel Eglwysbach, Berw Road. Built in 1889, this highly conspicuous building by the River Taff has walls of red brick and Corinthian half-columns. It was named Eglwysbach Memorial Chapel after Revd John Evans, who was known as Eglwys Bach from the place of his birth in North Wales. In the vestibule is a brick which Revd Evans brought back from Palestine. It is now home to a doctor's surgery.

Left: Sardis Chapel, which was built in 1834 and rebuilt in 1852. Sardis is the mother church of Seion Welsh Congregational church and the former English Congregational church – now the United church – on Gelliwastad Road and holds services in Welsh.

Below: Tabernacl Chapel, Bridge Street. The chapel was designed by the minister, Dr E. Roberts, and built in 1861. It is now home to Pontypridd Museum.

Carmel Chapel, Graigwen. There was a proliferation of Nonconformist chapels, where Welsh was the main language of worship, after 1810, when Carmel Chapel was built on Graigwen. It was the resting place of national anthem composer Evan James.

The interior of Carmel Chapel. The chapel was demolished in 1969 and Plas Carmel flats built on the site; the remains of Evan James were re-interred at Ynysangharad War Memorial Park in July 1973.

The Old School, Mill Street. It was opened in July 1874 and demolished in October 1912.

Pontypridd schools. The history of the Pontypridd Grammar School was dominated by Rhys Morgan, the first headmaster. In 1890, he opened the Heath School (the Academy) on Gelliwastad Road. The name was probably connected to the philanthropic activities of the local landowner, George Thomas 'The Heath'. The first pupil registered at the Heath was Oswal Davies, who in 1901 bought up the business of Matthews the chemist in the Arcade. Following the passing of the Welsh Intermediate Education Act in 1889, plans went ahead to set up a new school. By July 1891, progress was being made, with Lord Tredegar supplying two acres of land as a site and workmen of the Great Western Colliery donating £100, along with colliers from Ynysybwl.

Pontypridd Boys' Grammar School, known as 'the school on the hill'. Ignatius Williams, stipendiary magistrate, officially opened the Pontypridd County School, later the Grammar School, on 25 September 1896. By June 1897, there were 105 boys and 66 girls on the school roll, with six travelling such a distance that they lived in 'approved lodgings'. At the outset, the annual fees were fixed at £3 and for music studies £1 11s 6d. At first, Rhys Morgan's salary was £150 per annum, plus a capitation fee of £1 10s on each of his first 100 pupils, bringing his income to £300 per year. His staff consisted of the likes of Catherine E. Bedford, William Henry Rees (Soapy) and E.J. Dungate. After a long and successful history, Pontypridd Boys' Grammar School became Coedylan Comprehensive School in 1973. Its motto was 'Effort in Pursuit of Success'.

Pontypridd Girls' Grammar School. When Pontypridd Grammar School was twelve years old, it was found necessary to plan the building of a new school for girls. In September 1908, a committee was formed and land purchased at Llanover Estate in Treforest. The school was officially opened on 15 September 1913 by James Roberts JP, chairman of the Pontypridd board of governors.

three

A Cultural Capital

Evan James (Ieuan ap Iago, 1809-78). Born on 11 February 1809 in Eglwysilan, he was one of eleven children. The family later moved to the Ancient Druid Inn at Argoed. A weaver and wool merchant by profession, he moved to Pontypridd in November 1847 to run a woollen mill on Mill Street. He married Elizabeth Jones of Rhymney and the couple had seven children, the eldest being James. Evan and his son James composed the Welsh national anthem, 'Hen Wlad fy Nhadau' ('Land of My Fathers') in 1856. Evan was a poet and it is believed that he wrote the words after his brother, Daniel, had emigrated to America. He wrote the verses to explain why he could not leave his homeland. His son James composed the tune. The song was published in *Gems of Welsh Melody* (1860) and soon became extremely popular.

James James (Iago ap Ieuan, 1832-1902). James worked in his father's woollen mill before opening a public house in the town – and another in Mountain Ash – in 1873. He married Cecilia Miles and the couple had five children. A harpist and musician, who also earned a living playing in the inns of Pontypridd, he composed the tune of the Welsh national anthem while apparently walking along the banks of the River Rhondda in January 1856. At first it was known as 'Glan Rhondda' ('The Banks of the Rhondda'). Some believe the words were written before James composed the melody, which was based on an old harp instrumental composition, and others believe that the melody was composed before the words. The most likely story is that father and son got together on the night of James' walk and wrote the first verse, with the next two verses being completed on the following day. 'Glan Rhondda' was performed for the first time in the vestry of Capel Tabor, in Maesteg, by a singer called Elizabeth John from Pontypridd, and it soon became popular in the locality.

'Hen Wlad Fy Nhadau' manuscript, 1856. This is the only piece in the manuscript where James is noted as the composer and the composition date is clearly marked as January 1856. The song's popularity spread after the Llangollen Eisteddfod in 1858. Thomas Llewelyn of Aberdare won a competition for an unpublished collection of Welsh airs that included 'Glan Rhondda'. The adjudicator of the competition, Owain Alaw, asked for permission to include 'Glan Rhondda' in his publication, *Gems of Welsh Melody* (1860). This volume, which gave 'Glan Rhondda' its more famous title, 'Hen Wlad Fy Nhadau', was sold in large quantities. It was given large prominence in the National Eisteddfod in Bangor in 1874 and was sung by one of the leading singers of the day, Robert Rees (Eos Morlais).

The memorial to Evan James and James James in Ynysangharad War Memorial Park. Schoolmaster Rhys Morgan initiated a memorial fund to honour the composers. On 23 July 1930, Lord Treowen, watched by some 10,000 people, unveiled the memorial. Designed by Sir William Goscombe John, it consists of two bronze figures. They are a woman, representing poetry, and a male harpist, representing music, and are set on a plinth of blue pennant stone from Craig-yr-Hesg quarry.

The new Town Hall, with a seating capacity of 1,700, was built in 1890 at a cost of £5,000, and in the same year a public library and the Royal Clarence Theatre (later renamed the New Theatre) opened its doors. To set the seal on its new-found status, the town played host to the National Eisteddfod of 1893.

Opposite above: The ceremony to unveil the statue to Evan and James James. James' son Taliesin James (1856–1938), a lecturer at the Welsh College of Music and Drama, played the harp at the ceremony. The stone on the memorial bears a medallion of father and son and an inscription, in both Welsh and English. It says, 'Evan James and James James (1809–78, 1832–1902) father and son of Pontypridd who, inspired by a deep and tender love of their native land, united poetry and song and gave to Wales her national hymn Hen Wlad Fy Nhadau.' Afterwards, a procession went to Carmel Chapel.

Opposite below: A memorial tablet to Evan James and James James unveiled on 17 September 1931 by Hopkin Morgan JP. It was displayed in Mill Street, where Evan ran his woollen factory. The tablet was replaced by a new plaque in 1968.

The Town Hall, 1952. Preparations were under way for the annual police boxing championship held there throughout the 1950s.

The new Town Hall replaced a smaller hall, which was built in 1885 for £1,600 and seated 700. The smaller hall was known as the Lesser Town Hall and Welsh composer Dr Jospeh Parry (of 'Myfanwy' fame) lectured there in 1899 on the great masters of music.

Left: Owen Morgan, better known as Morien (1836-1921). Rhondda-born Morien settled in Glyntaff at a house known as Ashgrove and was the local journalist for the *Western Mail.* He specialised in the reporting of mining disasters, of which there were many and to which his florid style was well suited. He wrote from around 1870 until his death in 1921 about the local traditions of Druidism, the remnants of which he found in the oral traditions of the valleys of South Wales. Something of a local character himself, Morien was closely associated with Myfyr Morganwg (Evan Davies). Under the influence of the fictions of Iolo Morganwg, Morien wrote a number of books, which include *Pabell Dafydd* (1889), about the Druids, *Kimmerian Discoveries,* on the alleged Chaldean origins of the Welsh, *A Guide to the Gorsedd* and *A History of Pontypridd and the Rhondda Valleys* (1903). The latter, described by R.T. Jenkins as 'an odd jumble of Druidism, mythology, topography, local history and biography', is one of the most unreliable local history books of the time.

Below: The Pontypridd Royal Welsh Ladies' Choir, better known as the Madam Muriel Jones Choir, pictured by the bridges prior to their performance for the Duke and Duchess of Kent in Cardiff, October 1937. Founded in Treforest in 1927, they earned a great reputation for performing for almost thirty years – usually in traditional Welsh costume. During this time, they sang for royalty on twenty occasions, including performances for Princess Helena Victoria in Pontypridd in July 1929, the Duke and Duchess of Kent in 1937 and the Duke (later George VI) and Duchess of York at Windsor.

Stuart Burrows. Born in William Street, Cilfynydd in 1933, the 'King of Mozart' began his working career as a teacher but his magnificent talent as a tenor soon brought him enduring fame and good fortune. His recitals included works by Mozart, Beethoven, Berlioz, Schubert, Sullivan, Adams, Tippet, Tchaikovsky, Mallote, Mahler, Offenbach and Handel. He earned worldwide recognition for being adept at oratorios and operas, specialising in Puccini, Verdi, Donizetti and Mozartiano repertoire. In 1963, he debuted in Cardiff at the Welsh National Opera as Ismael in Verdi's *Nabucco* and, in 1967, his phenomenal performance during the Athens Festival brought him international acclaim. The well-crafted version of Igor Stravinsky's *Oedipus Rex* (which he performed at the request of the composer) was certain evidence of Stuart being one of the world's finest lyric tenors of all time. He also enjoyed his own BBC television series called *Stuart Burrows Sings*. Stuart performed at a variety of the best-known opera houses throughout the world. In New York, he has been accompanied by the talents of Sir Georg Solti, Zubin Mehta, Seiji Ozawa, Leonard Bernstein and Eugene Ormandy, among others, at the prestigious Carnegie Hall. He has also appeared in major roles at the Metropolitan Opera in New York City for more consecutive seasons than any British singer.

Beverley Humphreys. Born in Maesycoed, the daughter of a music teacher, she reached the finals of the Cinzano Opera Competition in Covent Garden. Although she didn't win, the Welsh National Opera recognised her talent. An audition followed and, at twenty-three, she first appeared as Rosina in *The Barber of Seville*, a part she has performed many times, while other roles have included Carmen, Santuzza and Amneris. She was firmly based in the world of opera, gracing the stage at the Royal Festival Hall and the Royal Albert Hall for the Queen and Prince Philip and spending more than ten years working in New York. She presented her own BBC radio show and, in 1992, went down in rugby history as the first Welsh singer allowed on the hallowed turf of the old Cardiff Arms Park to lead the Welsh team in singing the national anthem.

Sir Geraint Evans. Born in William Street, Cilfynydd in 1922, he was surrounded by music from birth. His father conducted the Pontypridd Male Choir and his mother, who died when he was a boy, was also a singer. The young Geraint was a talented pianist and violinist, and also sang in local productions. He left school at fourteen to work as a window-dresser in Pontypridd. He carried on performing as an amateur until the outbreak of the Second World War, when he joined the RAF but ended up in the music department of the British Forces Network, performing regularly on the radio. The Austrian bass singer Theo Hermann heard him and gave him lessons. It was through Hermann's contacts that he auditioned at the Royal Opera House, Covent Garden on his return. He joined the company in 1947 and quickly progressed to perform Figaro when he was only twenty-six. Many consider his greatest role to be that of Verdi's Falstaff, which he sang in opera houses across the world, complete with 30lbs of foam padding! Another defining moment came in 1960 when he was asked to perform Figaro at La Scala in Milan, under the baton of the great Herbert von Karajan. He was the first British singer to have performed at La Scala in thirty-five years. In March 1964, he travelled to New York for a debut at The Met, in a production of *Falstaff* directed by Zeffirelli. The conductor was Leonard Bernstein and the audience response was phenomenal. He died in 1992 and on the day of his funeral, hundreds of mourners lined the streets of Aberaeron to pay their last respects to one of the world's great opera singers.

Gillian Humphreys. Encouraged to take to the stage at the age of nine, she developed her own inimitable style of singing and studying at the Royal Academy of Music, working with Sir Tyrone Guthrie in California and then becoming principal soprano with the D'Oyle Carte Opera Company. Born in Long Row, Treforest before moving to nearby New Park Terrace, she attended Pontypridd Girls' Grammar School and enjoyed her first professional concert in Pontypridd with Stuart Burrows, performing Mendelssohn's *St Paul* with the Pontypridd Choral Society. A regular performer with the Glyndebourne Festival Opera and the Welsh National Opera, Ms Humphreys' career on the West Coast of the United States saw her perform at the Californian Pops Concerts with Nelson Riddle and appear in TV shows with Johnny Carson and Merv Griffin. Back home in the UK, she has made guest appearances on TV and in concert with Dick Emery, Morecambe and Wise, the Two Ronnies, Stanley Baxter, Ken Dodd, Bruce Forsyth, John Inman and Max Bygraves. She now runs the Concordia Foundation from her London home, encouraging the musical talents of young people throughout the country.

Opposite above: Côr Meibion Pontypridd. The choir began in November 1949, when a small gathering of nineteen men met with a view to forming a choir. Rehearsals began immediately at the YMCA, which was also known as Pontypridd Educational Settlement Hall (the Shelley Hall). The choir was known as the Pontypridd Educational Settlement Male Choir. Their first concert, in June 1950, was given for the Cilfynydd Old Age Pensioners Association. They began competing the following year, taking part in the Llanharan Eisteddfod, winning the first prize of £40. In June 1956, the choir made its first recording for the BBC, which was used in a programme celebrating the centenary of the composition of 'Hen Wlad Fy Nhadau' and the bicentenary of the building of the Old Bridge. These celebrations also included a major concert in the Town Hall, where the choir sang with Victoria Elliott, Constance Shacklock, Rowland Jones and Geraint Evans. In June 1959, the choir sang in the marquee in Ynysangharad Park with Stuart Burrows. The annual concert of 1959 was held in November and the soloists were Geraint Evans and Harry Secombe.

Opposite below: Côr Meibion Pontypridd. Dorothy Davies-Ingram joined the choir as an accompanist in 1964 and carried out that role for twelve years, before becoming musical director for thirteen years then returning to the post of accompanist. Pontypridd's twinning with the German town of Nurtingen began in 1964 and the choir have long-lasting links with the choir Liederkrantz Oberensingen. In 1973, Marlene Dietrich asked the choir to sing for her and this led to an invitation to give a fifteen-minute spot on her show at the New Theatre, Cardiff. In 1984, the choir purchased Mount Tabor Chapel in Vaughan Street, Pwllgwaun as their rehearsal room.´

Gwilym T. Jones. A native of Cwmparc, in the Rhondda, his
greatest success was enjoyed as conductor of Côr Meibion
Pontypridd and the Royal Welsh Male Choir. He later lived
in Wood Street, Cilfynydd until his death, at the age of
sixty-five, in 1952. His brother was bandmaster of the Parc
and Dare Band and Mr Jones had his first piano lesson at
the age of six. He was trained by Professor J. T. Jones and
received instruction in singing and piano throughout his
teenage years. From 1920 to 1939, he taught both subjects
and at the age of seventeen was invited to become conductor
of the Cwmparc Male Voice Choir. Under his guidance, it
flourished and in 1910 he joined the successful Royal Welsh
Male Choir as accompanist, before becoming conductor.
As their maestro, he made eleven appearances before royalty
and two tours were made in South Africa. Then, in 1926,
he came to Pontypridd with the task of training the 160
voices of the original Pontypridd and District Male Choir.
In 1928, he also took on the additional duty of conducting
the Llanharan Male Voice Choir. Mr Jones also conducted
the Cilfynydd Choral Society with his trademark baton – an
unusual silver-plated instrument with a telescopic point,
which fitted in his pocket. It was presented to him following
a win at a semi-national contest in London. Following the
reformation of the Pontypridd YMCA Male Voice Choir
in 1948, he became its conductor and remained in the post
until his death.

Tom Jones, seen here with Elvis Presley, c. 1968. The
superstar began life as Treforest-born Tom Woodward,
who was struck down by tuberculosis and bedridden for
almost a year, before channelling his energies into music.
At the age of sixteen, he left school and worked nights in
a paper mill. He became the lead singer of Tommy Scott
and the Senators, a local sensation. Tom was spotted by
London-based manager Gordon Mills, who recognised
his potential. His first single, 'It's Not Unusual', become a
worldwide smash, followed closely by the likes of 'Delilah'
and 'The Green, Green Grass of Home'. It was the
beginning of a Welsh legend.

PONTYPRIDD
WAR MEMORIAL
YNYSANGHARAD PARK
FOR THE TOWN.

THE horrors of the Great War are over, the Dragon of Militarism, let us hope, has been slain, and its carcase finally laid in the dust. We may not, we dare not, forget the price that was paid. Scores of the lads of our own town fought, bled, and died to win for us all the freedom we enjoy.

LET the sweet instincts of our nature find expression to their gratitude in blessing our town for all ages with an emblem of freedom, beauty, and service in the gift of a Park for its people.

DUTY calls for a contribution from each. To those who have been spared the atrocities of war let it be a thank-offering to the gallant boys who stood in the breach; to those who endured the hardship of the camp and the hazard of the field, let it be an acknowledgment of thanks for sparing their lives; and to all let it be a noble tribute to the illustrious dead. As when in the flesh they challenged Death to do its worst, and emerged victorious, so now from their vantage ground beyond the veil their spirits invoke us to change the face of this old world of ours by sinking self in noble deeds of love and gratitude.

"Free Press," Taff-street, Pontypridd.

An advertisement for Ynysangharad War Memorial Park. Ynysangharad Fields were acquired by the PUDC in 1919 and opened on 6 August 1923 by Field Marshal Lord Allenby as a park in memory of those who made the ultimate sacrifice. Grand memorial gates of iron, which are no longer there, stood at the main entrance of the park in Bridge Street. The park gleamed like a jewel in the town for people seeking sports activities, rest and relaxation or walks in the spacious greenery.

Taff River, Bridge & Park, Pontypridd

General View of Pontypridd (showing Park and Mountains)

The Avenue, Ynysangharad War Memorial Park. A magnificent avenue of trees, planted in the early 1930s alongside the new tennis courts, led from the 1923 concrete bridge over the River Taff.

Opposite above: The bridge from Taff Street to Ynysangharad Park. The Scudamore family owned a slaughterhouse at the rear of Taff Street. Allan Scudamore was managing director of the Pontypridd Pure Ice Stores in Gas Lane at the time when the hundreds of lambs and turkeys for the Pontypridd market and town shops were placed in the cold storage. For many years, their well-known family butcher's shop occupied the site on the corner of Market Street and Church Street. During the war, Allan was a popular Master of Ceremonies at local dance halls. When he was a boy, he lived in Ynysangharad House, a large building with a small farmyard and outbuildings set in Ynysangharad Fields. The house was occupied in Victorian times by George William Lenox and Lewis Gordon Lenox JP, partners at the chainworks, and by the firm's manager George James Penn. The house (along with nearby Kenver House) was demolished in the 1930s and a clinic was built on part of the site.

Opposite below: A general view of Ynysangharad War Memorial Park and Pontypridd. The island in midstream was known as Ynys Angharad (Angharad's Island) or Ynys y Cariadon (Lovers' Island).

The jewel in the crown of Pontypridd, Ynysangharad War Memorial Park was the venue for the celebrated Tom Jones 65th Birthday Concert. It marked a triumphant return for the superstar as he performed on the green, green grass of home for the first time in forty years.

The sunken garden, Ynysangharad War Memorial Park. At the outbreak of the war, leaflets in a Dig for Victory campaign urged everyone to cultivate allotments for growing vegetables. An area of the cricket field in the park was given up for the campaign and the vegetables were supplied mainly to the restaurant in the Tabernacl Chapel vestry.

The Walk, Ynysangharad War Memorial Park. Lawns and flower beds were delicately planted and tended and, later, a walled sunken garden added to its attractions.

Ynysangharad War Memorial Park and the bandstand. The first open-air community hymn-singing service by the united churches of Pontypridd was held in June 1943 in front of the cricket pavilion. More than 1,000 people turned up in the evening to sing under conductor W.D. Evans of Maerdy.

The bandstand in Ynysangharad War Memorial Park. In 1953, the Queen and the Duke of Edinburgh, accompanied by other members of the royal party, spoke from the bandstand during their royal visit. The Lord Lieutenant presented Pontypridd's leading citizen, Arthur Brown, the chairman of the District Council, and the Town Clerk, John Hilton. The Queen remarked how impressed she was at the beauty of Ynysangharad Park, while the Duke chatted about the Test Match with Mr Hilton, a keen cricketer. Accompanying the royal couple were Sir David Maxwell Fyfe, Home Secretary, and the Minister for Welsh Affairs. Also Sir Harold Campbell and Sir Alan Lascelles, the Queen's Private Secretary.

The bowling green and tennis courts, Ynysangharad War Memorial Park. The bowling greens were opened in May 1924 and new greens with many improvements opened in April 1929. In July 1945, the Pontypridd Bowls Club won the championship of the Cardiff Municipal Bowls League in a game with Heath, in Roath Park, Cardiff. Herbert (Bert) Hughes was then the secretary of the Pontypridd club.

Cricket Pavilion, Pontypridd Park.

The cricket pavilion, Ynysangharad War Memorial Park. Pontypridd has nurtured many leading cricket players over the years, most notably Bernard Hedges, who played for Glamorgan between 1950 and 1967. During this time, he amassed over 17,000 runs in first-class cricket and, in 1963, scored the county's first ever hundred in one-day cricket.

The children's swimming pool, Ynysangharad War Memorial Park. A familiar splashing ground for hundreds of local children and their parents.

The children's swimming pool, 1972. Childhood memories are certainly made of warm summer days like this at the paddling pool in Ponty park.

The children's swimming pool, c. 1935. This is the pool viewed from the other direction, with plenty of young families enjoying a paddle.

The swimming pool in Ynysangharad War Memorial Park. Affectionately known as Ponty Baths, 600,000 gallons of water were pumped through the purification plant every twenty-four hours. During the 1950s, it was billed as the largest open-air swimming pool in Wales. It was here that great swimmers like Jenny James and Roy Hunt learned their craft. Although now in a sorry state, the lido is in fact a Grade II listed building.

Ynysangharad War Memorial Park during the flooding of December 1960. Despite being a recognised flood plain and therefore prone to flooding from the River Taff, a health and day centre were built close to the park gates on Bridge Street.

The visit of Princess Louise, 23 July 1909. The Fountain in Taff Street was transformed into a rock garden and a giant bouquet, while a profusion of flowers, ribbons, flags and bunting adorned the trams and streets of Pontypridd and the villages for the visit of the sister of King Edward VII. A twenty-one-gun salute was fired from the Ivor Arms field. Trams were also specially decorated in June 1911 for the Coronation of King George V and Queen Mary, who stopped off briefly at Pontypridd station in June 1912 while on a visit to the Rhondda and Merthyr.

The opening of the Young Men's Christian Association by Sir Clifford Cory MP on 29 September 1910. The YMCA was opened in a bid to get young men off the streets. Sports and other social activities were organised on a regular basis to offer them an alternative to crime and alcohol. During the same year, the Pontypridd Labour Exchange was also opened in the town.

Metropolitan Police from London guarding Taff Street near the New Inn, December 1910. The miners' disputes of 1910-11 in the Rhondda were due to the change in the wage system that owners were trying to introduce. In October 1910, there was a dispute at Cambrian Combine and 800 men were locked out. In November 1910, 12,000 miners went on strike. Violence broke out as the strikers stopped other miners going to work, and bitterness led to riots in Tonypandy. One miner died after a blow to the head, thought to be from a police truncheon. The Home Secretary, Winston Churchill, sent troops into the area to keep the peace. The miners returned to work in October 1911. The same miners went on trial at Pontypridd Court and police were called in to ensure peace was maintained in the town.

Metropolitan Police at Graigwen Hill, December 1910. Members of the Metropolitan Police remained on hand to ensure that no riots broke out in the market town similar to those at Tonypandy at the time of the trial in the local courthouse. There were several blockades on the main roads through Pontypridd, particularly along Taff Street and at the entrance to the railway station.

An open-air religious meeting at the Pontypridd railway station approach, c.1905. These occasions were due to the religious fervour which swept the valleys during the Methodist Revival of 1904.

Jubilee decorations in Taff Street, 1935. The streets of the town were decorated for the Silver Jubilee celebrations of King George V and Queen Mary.

Above: Jubilee decorations in Market Street, 1935. The Market Company made sure their headquarters were well decorated for the festivities. This picture shows the entrance to the market alongside Scudamore's butchers on the corner of Church Street.

Left: Royal visit, Mill Street, 1936. On 18 November 1936, King Edward VIII visited Pontypridd. He came to the Ministry of Labour training centre in Mill Street. Within a month, the King had abdicated to marry American divorcee Wallis Simpson.

The unveiling of the 5th Welch war memorial by Viscount Allenby on 6 August 1923. The memorial was unveiled on the Common in remembrance of Pontypridd's 28 officers, 3 warrant officers, 51 NCOs and 279 men of the battalion who died in the First World War.

A Camp 2nd Battalion, Pontypridd Home Guard, 17 May 1941. Pontypridd Home Guard (2nd Glamorgan Battalion) had two full-time officers, Captain Ernest L. Beech MC and Captain W.A. Jacob. The sector commander was Colonel W. Lester Lewis, a local magistrate's clerk. The third anniversary of the founding of the Home Guard was celebrated with a parade of more than 1,200 men through the streets of the town.

VE day parade, 1945. Victory celebrations held in Pontypridd reflected the jubilation felt at the end of the Second World War. Crowds packed Market Street, the Square and Taff Street for 3 p.m. on Tuesday 8 May 1945, to hear Winston Churchill's broadcast amplified from Rediffusion Ltd at No. 10 Market Street – now the home of the *Observer*. Some time later, a victory parade was held, with bands of the Air Training Corps, Sea Cadets and Army Cadets marching through the town.

The visit of Queen Elizabeth II and the Duke of Edinburgh to Pontypridd, 9 July 1953. 'I wish I could stay longer,' the Queen told Arthur Brown JP, chairman of the Pontypridd Council, shortly before she left Ynysangharad Park during her tour of Wales. The Queen, accompanied by the Duke of Edinburgh, was greeted by 40,000 well-wishers during their visit. The crowds had gathered in an orderly fashion for more than four hours before the royal couple made an appearance at 2.35 p.m., when their car turned into the park from Cardiff Road. They walked through the park to the tune of the Welsh national anthem. The band of the Welch Regiment also performed. Comprising the massed choirs which sang under conductor Gwilym Jones were the Pontypridd Male Choir, Pontypridd Choral Society, Pontypridd Operatic Society and the Calvary Chapel Choral Society. Marshalling the crowds were 500 special police under Supt Arthur Morris and the 5th Battalion, Welch Regiment. As the royal couple left, following the thirteen-minute stop, Gillian Alexander, aged twelve, presented Her Majesty with a bouquet of yellow rosebuds and lilies-of-the-valley.

A celebration programme from 1956, a year to remember in Pontypridd history, as it marked the centenary of the composition of 'Hen Wlad Fy Nhadau' and the bicentenary of the building of William Edward's favourite bridge. Schools, choirs, churches, chapels and Rotary clubs all got together to make arrangements. The *Observer* sponsored an essay-writing competition and Sir Geraint Evans held a concert in the town, attended by the Earl and Countess of Harewood. The BBC flocked to Ponty and the park was packed for seven full days. The main event began on 3 June, with a service of celebration at the bandstand in the park. An evening hymn-singing concert saw the band of the 5th Battalion, Welch Regiment perform under Lt-Col. C.H. Allen. The Old Age Pensioners Association held a Festival of Song in a marquee and one of the most memorable moments was the Beating the Retreat by the Welch Regiment band, followed by a full concert in the open air. There was a Welsh Day and a Noson Lawen. On Thursday 7 June, all eyes were turned on Taff Vale Park, with the Pontypridd Secondary School's sports day followed by a concert featuring the Boys' Grammar School pupils in Ynysangharad Park. The festivities continued with a major celebrity concert in the Town Hall Theatre, featuring Geraint Evans, Constance Shacklock, Victoria Elliott and Rowland Jones.

The visit of Diana, Princess of Wales to Pontypridd, 1981. Diana displayed the common touch from the start in a visit to Pontypridd in October 1981, her first to Wales since marrying Prince Charles in July of that year.

Above left: Freddie Welsh (1886-1927). Pontypridd's Frederick Hall Thomas was the son of a tradesman and was sent to Long Ashton College, a public school in Bristol. He suffered respiratory problems and when he was sixteen he left industrial South Wales for the cleaner air of Canada. It was there he started to box. He then moved to Philadelphia and started to fight for a living. He won the British title in 1909, beating Johnnie Summers on points. In 1913, he married Fanny Weston and a year later Welsh became world champion. His rivals called him the Snowflake Puncher, claiming Welsh could not hit hard, although he scored many knockout victories. His speciality, however, was a devastating kidney punch which is now illegal. Opinions are divided on why he changed his name from Fred Thomas to Freddie Welsh. One view is that he did not want his mother to find out he had become a boxer. Another opinion, and the most likely, is that when he first arrived on the other side of the Atlantic he was asked, 'Are you Welsh?' and adopted it as his new surname. He earned a fortune as the greatest lightweight boxer the world had seen and set up a luxury health farm in New Jersey following his retirement from the ring in 1922, but it proved a disastrous venture and Welsh lost everything. He died of a heart attack, a lonely and penniless man in a bleak New York apartment, in 1927, aged forty-one.

Above right: The Moody brothers Jack, Frank and Glen of Pontypridd. Ted E. Lewis, manager of boxers Frank Moody and Jimmy Wilde, once said, 'Each of the nine Welshmen who won British titles were born and bred within a twenty-mile radius of the Fountain in Taff Street. If ever boxing should determine the point, Pontypridd would easily be entitled to the description of "capital of Wales".' Frank Moody was known affectionately as the Pontypridd Puncher. From the age of eleven, Frank was working in the pits, until his boxing success turned him professional in the 1920s. He knocked out Tommy Milligan in fifty-eight seconds in Glasgow in 1928 and beat everyone in Wales near his weight. Frank earned titles as British middleweight and light heavyweight champion. Glen's first fight was an exhibition bout held to raise money to feed hungry children during the miners' strike of 1926. He later became Welsh middleweight and light heavyweight champion.

Jenny James. On 16 August 1951, Jenny Eileen James became the first Welsh person to swim the English Channel. The twenty-four-year-old Pontypridd girl swum from France to England in thirteen hours and fifty-five minutes. Her achievement won her a place in the record book of the Channel Swimming Association. She was just seven when she first found her talent for swimming and it led her into a career as a swimming coach and a lifeguard that saw her save more than 100 lives. She became a lifeguard at Ponty Baths and it was a regular venue for her physical training during the early years. It was a far cry from the icy waters of the English Channel, which she swam from Calais to Dover. She had already broken the Bristol Channel record twelve months earlier, becoming the first woman to swim it both ways. Jenny, who lived in Wood Road, Treforest, was greased down with lanolin for protection and warmth as she left Calais. Following a rowing boat carrying her father and assistant Bill Woodman, she listened for instruction. A mile from St Margaret's Bay, her father clapped to let her know how close she was and she sprinted away, reaching the beach at 9.30 p.m. A trip to customs was followed by a hot bath and a relaxing sleep but at 3 a.m. she returned to the beach to see the spot on which she had landed.

The welcoming party for Jenny James at Pontypridd, 1951. Jenny James continued her swimming career following the Channel swim but became an assistant matron at a boys' school in Cheltenham to fund her overseas trips. Her later sporting achievements include swimming the River Loire in Nantes, France in 1955, the Egypt race, also in 1955, and the Suez Canal marathon in 1963 and 1964.

The Taff Street Dash. The 100 yard sprint along Taff Street first took place in 1959. After seventeen years, the series was halted, although it was revived for one year in 1991.

Pontypridd Cricket Club. The club was formed in May 1870 and played its first match, against the Publicans Eleven, in the grounds of Gelliwastad House. Pontypridd had a strong and stylish cricket team in 1897, when the Glamorgan Cricket League was established. In the 1896 season, the club was undefeated in the league and won the league championship. The club moved to Ynysangharad Park in 1924. Some seasons later, the club affiliated to the Glamorgan County Cricket Club, who had paid half the £800 cost of a new pavilion, and the first county match was played in the park, with Derbyshire the opponents.

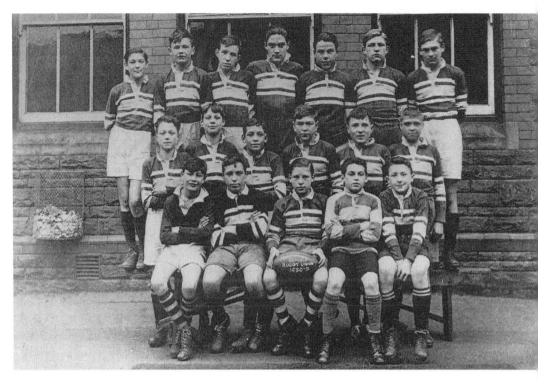

Pontypridd Schools Rugby Union 1930/31. The first meeting of the Welsh Schools Rugby Union was held in Cardiff in 1903. Cardiff School played their first inter-town game against Pontypridd away on 21 March 1903. Cardiff won by a try to nil.

Bryn Davies, the Welsh Powderhall Sprint champion, 1929. The world-famous race took place at Taff Vale Park – the top spot for Welsh sporting events – before the Second World War. Athletes from Canada, USA, South Africa, Australia and Tasmania spent weeks aboard ships sailing to the UK in the hope of carrying off Wales' most prestigious foot race. The period from 1903, when the first Powderhall was run, until its demise in 1934 was undoubtedly one of the most colourful, dramatic and exciting times in the history of Welsh sport. In a meeting of 21 July 1903, it was decided to hold a £100 sprint and a couple of minor events. By the following year, 5,000 people turned up. For the first time, all 100 entrants were Welsh in the 1929 race and the winner was Bryn Davies of Pontypridd. According to reports, Bryn 'ran like a man possessed', with Treforest man Les Thomas coming second. Bryn's winning time was the fastest recorded on the grass track. However, he became disillusioned with the sport and hung up his spikes, later to become a foreman plater with the National Coal Board. He died, aged eighty-two, in 1990.

Above left: Swimmer Roy Hunt. Born in Coedpenmaen, he had his first swimming lesson at the age of seven from his father at Ynysangharad Park in 1943. He wanted to become a member of the swimming club and juniors paid half a crown at the start of the season, which ran from June to September. There were plenty of swimming coaches on hand, like Ted Pritchard, Herbert Langley, Ted Payne, Frank Williams, David Rogers and Mr Rogers Senior. Devoted to the swimming club, Roy realised he was at his best as a long-distance swimmer. In June 1957, a swimming club was formed in Yorkshire and a 10½ mile championship race took place on Lake Windermere. Organised by the British Long-Distance Swimming Association, Roy decided to enter. The swim had been completed using the breaststroke by John Humphries in 1933, in a time of ten hours and four minutes. Nobody had swum the lake using the breaststroke since, until Roy ventured into the water. There were twenty competitors and rowing boats were moored nearby with escorts but waves filled the escorts' boat and all of Roy's food and provisions were swept overboard. In worsening conditions and poor visibility, the only food he was offered was two boiled sweets. He came an admirable third in eight hours and two minutes, achieving a new best in the breaststroke.

Above right: Glyn Davies. The mercurial outside-half played for Wales on twelve occasions and played two of those games while still in Form Six at Pontypridd Grammar School. One of three children, his sisters were Marion and Brenda, who married operatic baritone Sir Geraint Evans. Glyn was born in 1927 and captained Pontypridd Boys' Grammar School rugby team, where he was also head boy. While still a pupil, he was picked to play outside-half for Wales. He also captained the Welsh Schoolboys' swimming pool team, Welsh Schoolboys' rugby team and even played for the youth side of Glamorgan Cricket Club. He also played rugby in the Army and later captained Cambridge University rugby team, while he was a student there, becoming the first freshman to play without a trial. In later years, he married Pontypridd-born Hilda Livesey and went on to become the director of Harvey's Bristol Cream before his untimely death due to a heart attack while in his late forties.

Pontypridd RFC 1897/98. Pontypridd Rugby Football Club was formed in 1876 and was sufficiently well established by March 1880 to be one of nine clubs that met at the Tenby Hotel, Swansea to discuss the formation of a national union. In 1886/87, the headquarters of the club was the Maltsters Arms and the club played its home matches at the Ynysangharad and Trallwn Fields. In 1890/91, the club moved to a field alongside the River Taff at Treforest and began the development of the famous Taff Vale Park. The final Welsh trial was held there in December 1892. The club then moved to the People's Park in Mill Street in 1901 and it stayed there for three seasons. Then, on 1 October 1904, it played Caerphilly in the first game on a new pitch at Ynysangharad Fields. Although the club later returned to Taff Vale Park for a short time, it was back at Ynysangharad by 1908 and stayed there for sixty-six years.

Pontypridd RFC, who played South Wales Police RFC in November 1952. Although Pontypridd played many games against the top Welsh clubs between the wars, much of the fixture list was composed of 'junior' clubs. The man chiefly responsible for steering Pontypridd through these difficult years was D.G. Williams, who was chairman for over thirty years. When games resumed after the Second World War, Pontypridd battled to maintain first-class status. There was also a constant battle with the local authorities to improve the facilities at Ynysangharad Park. The teams changed in the swimming baths, over 200 yards from the field, and there was no proper terracing or grandstand. Many Pontypridd players, then as now, came from the local schools out of the Pontypridd Youth XV (formed in 1954).

Pontypridd Rugby Club XV, 13 April 1963. For many years, the unofficial headquarters of the club was the Greyhound Inn but in the 1960/61 season it opened a new clubhouse, Park View, near the northern entrance to Ynysangharad Park, which remained its headquarters until May 1971. The new A470 trunk road meant that Pontypridd would have to move from its clubhouse and pitch. A new ground was developed at Pwllgwaun, in the area known as Dan's Muck Hole, after the colliery which used to be there. The new clubhouse at Pwllgwaun was opened on 18 January 1974 and was soon to be known to all of the rugby world simply as Sardis Road. The grandstand became available in February 1975, the dressing rooms in mid-March and the floodlights in late March, in a game against Ruthin.

Pontypridd RFC 1968. From left to right, back row: John Pope, Russell Jones, David Edwards, Bob Penberthy, Roy Hope, Colin Owen, Jeff Davies, Gareth Thomas, Bill Davey, Gareth Rees, Joe Smith. Front row: Dennis John, Arfon Jones (captain), Glyn James, Wyn Davies

Tommy David. Pontypridd born and bred, Tommy played for the town's schools and youth teams before progressing to the ranks of the Pontypridd seniors. A flanker, he made 404 appearances for the club between 1967 and 1981. He helped the club to three league championship crowns, before taking the high road to Llanelli, from where he gained international honours with Wales and the British Lions. Tommy's heroics on the Lions tour to New Zealand in 1971, and his part in plotting the demise of the same opponents for Llanelli and the Barbarians, were quite simply the stuff of legend. Tommy returned to Pontypridd in 1975, captaining the team to another two league championships. He later went on to play rugby league for the newly formed Cardiff Dragons, before retiring from the game and progressing to be a director with Pontypridd's long-standing sponsors, Buy as you View.

Pontypridd *v.* Waunarlwydd, February 1975. The 1975–81 period in the club's history was a golden era. In six seasons, the team played 326 games, winning 263 of them and drawing 7. The Australian touring team played at Sardis Road in December 1981 and Pontypridd narrowly lost a titanic struggle by three points to six. The decision was made in 1988 to set up a league system in Welsh club rugby, to start in 1990/91 season. Pontypridd had the players and coaches to get into the top flight. Two players who would make the greatest impact on Pontypridd rugby over the next decade made their first appearances in the 1989/90 season: Dale 'The Chief' McIntosh made his first appearance on 11 November 1989 and Nel Jenkins came in on 14 April 1990.

Bob Penberthy. If one person could ever be set as an icon for Pontypridd RFC, the one who stands head and shoulders above the rest is the 'bionic elbow', Bob Penberthy. Following his debut against Penarth on 1 November 1961, Bob went on to play an incredible 877 games for Pontypridd before 1985, a feat that will surely never be surpassed. Bob represented the Barbarians and toured various destinations such as Canada and Germany with his club but mostly spent his time, week in week out, plying his trade in the rough-house environment of the line-outs of Welsh club rugby. After retirement, Bob continued his work as a linesman with South Wales Electricity, with his Saturdays devoted unfailingly to following the club which he served with such great distinction for so many years.

Tommy David's International XV, 1975. From left to right, back row: Cenydd Thomas (referee), Terry Andrews (trainer), David Duckham, Andy Ripley, Mervyn Davies, Chris Ralston, Mike Burton, Geoff Evans, Mr Drayton-Lewis (touch judge), Mr J.D. Samuel (touch judge). Front row: Tony Falkner, John J. Williams, Gareth Edwards, Phil Bennett, Tom David, Bobby Windsor, John Williams, Gerald Davies, Tony Neary.

Other local titles published by The History Press

Llantrisant Revisited
DEAN POWELL

This fascinating collection of over 200 old images pays tribute to the people who have proudly called Llantrisant their home. Commanding an outstanding setting on the crest of a hill, Llantrisant's splendour lies in its enchanting beauty and celebrated past. Bloodthirsty battles, pioneering acts of cremation and captured kings of England have all played a part in shaping the town, as have the generations of families who have lived here.

0 7524 3216 X

Catholics in Cardiff
JOHN O'SULLIVAN

In 1820 there were only three Catholics in Cardiff: two Irishmen and a businessman from Usk. Today there are nineteen Catholic parishes, one university chaplaincy, seven convents, fourteen Catholic primary schools, four Catholic secondary schools and one Catholic Independent School within the city boundaries. Compiled with over 200 photographs, Catholic Cardiff illustrates Catholic life in the city during the last century, including the annual Corpus Christi celebrations, events at the Cathedral, pilgrimages to Lourdes, as well as Papal visits, Catholic schools and first communion.

0 7524 3364 4

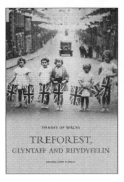

Treforest, Glyntaff and Rhydyfelin
RHODRI JOHN POWELL

This fascinating collection of over 200 old photographs traces the changes that have taken place in Treforest, Glyntaff and Rhydyfelin since the nineteenth century. The Treforest Industrial Estate and the South Wales and Monmouthshire School of Mines are featured and the influence of local figures such as Francis Crawshay and William Price recalled. Treforest, Glyntaff and Rhydyfelin will delight all those know this area of South Wales.

0 7524 3507 8

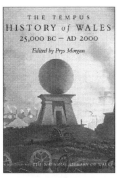

The Tempus History of Wales
PRYS MORGAN

Wales was at the heart of the Industrial Revolution, with towns like Merthyr Tydfil driving the engine of the British Empire. The cultural and social divide between modern, industrialised Wales and the traditional agricultural areas is explored within this comprehensive volume.

0 7524 1983 8

If you are interested in purchasing other books published by The History Press, or in case you have difficulty finding any of our books in your local bookshop, you can also place orders directly through our website
www.thehistorypress.co.uk

Printed in Great Britain
by Amazon